LIT FROM WITHIN

A LIFE POWERED BY THE HOLY SPIRIT

BY BRANDIE BARCLAY

PowerSoul, Lit from Within

For privacy reasons, some names, locations, and dates may have been changed.

Published with help from 100X Publishing, www.100xpublishing.com.

ISBN Paperback: 979-8-9958812-1-6
ISBN Hardcover: 979-8-9958812-0-9

Cover photo by Jamie Lindsay. Front cover design by Lissette Lent.

Dedicated to the woman who kept going

even when her soul was tired.

The one who knew there had to be more

and was brave enough to seek power for her soul.

"This book is a powerful callback to spiritual clarity in times of confusion. Through real life battles and hard-won testimony, Brandie leads readers into the truth of Scripture with depth, courage, and conviction. More than inspiration, this message brings practical activation, equipping believers to walk in discernment, exercise your authority in Christ, and mature in faith. A timely and necessary voice for those who refuse to remain spiritually passive and are ready to grow deeper in Christ."

—Kristie Sexton,
Campus Pastor at Dream City Church, Phoenix

"Most books share information...the good ones tell stories that reach the depths of our soul. Brandie is able to mine the depth and bring up gold! With her raw, candid, and down-to-earth voice, she does a deep dive and comes up with the oxygen that powers our soul and lights us from within...the Holy Spirit. So, rise up, brave one, and claim your authority. This book will shift your atmosphere!"

—Robin Gerblick,
Award-Winning Author

"PowerSoul peels back the layers and exposes a deep Spiritual connection to your inner power, true destiny and gives you permission through the holy spirit to be the amazing human you were meant to be! A must read!"

—Joe Courtney,
Former NBA Player, Chicago Bulls
Motivational Speaker & Author

"It is a true honor to introduce you to Brandie Barclay and the powerful message she carries in *PowerSoul*.

Brandie is a beautiful soul who has courageously walked out her journey with God—through challenges, through growth, and through deep places of breakthrough. What makes her story so impactful is that she has not only lived it, but she has taken the time to extract the strategic keys that now equip others.

As I've watched Brandie's life, I've seen a woman who chose transformation over staying stuck, truth over lies, and freedom over fear. She understands what it means to walk with the living God in real, everyday life, and she shares that journey with authenticity, joy, and wisdom.

This book will make you laugh, it will encourage your heart, and it will give you practical, powerful tools to move forward in your own walk with God. If you are in a season of transition, healing, or stepping into something new, the keys in this book will equip you for what lies ahead.

PowerSoul is not just a message, it's an impartation of faith, clarity, and Kingdom strategy.

I wholeheartedly recommend this book to every person who desires to live healed, walk closely with God, and step into the fullness of their calling."

—Cathy Greer,
Consultant, Speaker, Entrepreneur, Mentor
President of Mission Support Network

PowerSoul™

Power:

The ability or capacity to act, produce an effect, or influence outcomes.

Soul:

The inner part of a person–their mind, will, and emotions or the core of who they are.

PowerSoul:

A person whose inner life is led and strengthened by the power of God.

Not controlled by emotions, culture, or circumstances but anchored in truth and aligned with Him.

CONTENTS

FOREWORD

By Kari Lake

When Brandie Barclay walks into a room, something shifts.

I've seen it in prayer circles, political spaces, and on public platforms. She doesn't play church. She shows up with truth in her mouth and the fire of the Holy Spirit. When she speaks, you feel it.

Brandie and I didn't just become friends. We locked arms. We've prayed before rallies, stood together through battles, and cried out to God for this nation. I've watched her walk into rooms most people would avoid, always bringing something real. Something holy.

When I need truth, prayer, or someone to go to battle with, I call her. She's someone I lean on spiritually because she carries discernment, boldness, and conviction in a way that's rare.

What I love most about Brandie is that she's unshakably authentic. She'll look you in the eye, call you higher, and then pray with you. She's not chasing a platform. She wants to see people free.

That's why this book matters.

PowerSoul: Lit from Within isn't soft inspiration or Christian fluff. It's a call to rise. This is what it looks like when someone walks through fire with God and comes out lit, not burned.

In these pages, Brandie tells the truth about pain, obedience, deliverance, and trusting God when nothing makes sense. She doesn't water it down or wrap it in religious language. She says it straight, with humor and grace.

And she doesn't stop at her story. She calls you into yours.

This book will remind you who you are and what you carry. You'll learn to hear God clearly, move when He says move, and walk in the authority you've been given.

So, if you've ever felt overlooked, underqualified, too much, or not enough, you're in the right place. This book will meet you where you are, but it won't leave you there.

You are not invisible. You are not too late. You are not too broken.

You are a PowerSoul. And once you see it, everything changes.

—Kari Lake
Senior Advisor for the U.S. Agency for Global Media,
Former broadcast journalist and public figure

PREFACE

Voice in the Water

Zechariah 4:6:

Not by might nor by power, but by my Spirit, says the Lord Almighty.

Imagine Moses standing at the Red Sea, the water raging before him and Pharaoh's army pressing in from behind. Fear. Pressure. Panic.

God didn't ask Moses for a battle plan. He didn't ask him to fight the enemy off on his own.

God asked Moses to simply obey His instructions and use what was already in his hand—his faith in God (believing in the power and presence) and the anointing from God (supernatural empowerment).

And when Moses stretched out his staff, the water moved.

It was God who made a way where there was no way.

It was God who defeated the enemy.

In this painstaking journey of *trying* to write this book, God revealed this sweet reminder:

I wasn't meant to do *any* of this on my own.

Like Moses, I'm just a weak, flawed, unqualified someone who God has called to follow His voice. And in doing so, I became a

PowerSoul, unafraid and untamed for Christ.

This book isn't about eloquence or effort. It's about obedience. Moses didn't ask to lead; in fact, it terrified him. He told God, "I'm not gifted. I stutter. Who am I to stand before Pharaoh?" And what was God's response? God didn't hype him up with self-confidence. He didn't hand him a detailed plan. He simply said: "I AM."

It was never about who Moses was, and it's not about who I am or who you are either. **It has always been about who God is and what *He* can do.**

On my own, I'm ill-equipped. But by abiding in Jesus, by the power of the Holy Spirit, my life completely changed for the better. I learned that in obeying God I could stop striving, performing, and grinding through life. I could move mountains in faith.

This book is me stretching out my hand, putting my voice in the water, and defying the enemy's plans to silence me. It is my *yes* to God. Like Moses, even though my story is woven through these pages, it was never about me. It is about what happens when ordinary people obey God's promptings even while feeling weak and unqualified. It is about what happens when you say yes while resistance rises and pressure increases—when obedience becomes strength and God sets a fire in your soul that cannot be contained.

Earlier in my walk with God, I wandered. I circled the same mountains of insecurities, fears and "what ifs." I replayed the same arguments and carried discouragements that drained my energy and dimmed my confidence. I knew something had to shift but wasn't sure how to break the cycle.

The wilderness (as shown in the Bible) was meant to shape God's people, not become their permanent address. It was a place of refining, not a place of residence. God did not rescue us so we could continue circling old destructive patterns and rehearsing old doubts. He calls us forward. Not when we *feel* ready, but when we are willing. The moment we choose obedience over fear is the moment God's super touches our natural.

This is OUR story...mine and my best friend's, the Holy Spirit, who has turned my chaos into calm and my weakness to strength. He is the One who gives me the audacity to say yes to what looks impossible. Over and over He doesn't fail to part the seas in front of me. The stories in this book are my personal testimonies. These are God-given visions and modern-day parables of how God has transformed me and my life when I stopped fighting battles God never asked me to fight and started to follow His promptings instead.

I *get to.*

I have the privilege of partnering with the Master of all Masterminds every single day. But I didn't start there...I spent decades *trying hard* to be a "good Christian" and ended up bored, burned out, and frustrated.

Those days are over because now I understand that I don't need to keep earning what's already been given. And I don't need to know it all. I just need to trust and follow the One who knows.

And just like Moses, I am not the hero or the victim.

I am the saved.

1

POWER OF SURRENDER

Psalm 37:5:

Commit everything you do to the LORD.
Trust him, and he will help you.

The sun glistened across the salt water as I vigorously dug my hands and feet deep into the sand.

My friend and I had just been talking and laughing as we sloshed hip-deep back to shore when a giant wave crashed down on top of her. Knowing I was next, I covered my head, took a breath, and boom.

Like a ragdoll, I was thrown around in the unforgiving current. Pulled to the bottom, I landed on my butt and slid in the undertow. I clawed the sand for what felt like forever until I realized my efforts were in vain. Tired and powerless, panic left me as I considered my fate.

I might not make it out alive.

Thoughts of my parents filled my mind, knowing they would get the news that I drowned here on my senior trip in Hawaii. I prayed for God to save me.

Suddenly, the water shifted, releasing me from the quicksand. The light at the surface was my compass until I finally caught a breath.

In life, there is a supernatural pull. One force drags you under, screaming, "Push! Panic! Kick harder, loser!" The other draws you higher, whispering, "Be still. Surrender. Pursue the light. I've got you."

Obviously, I didn't die at 17, but that moment would be prophetic. For many years, I listened to the wrong voice. It pushed me harder and accused me of not being good enough as I scrambled to catch my breath.

There was a time when I was drowning in the "good" life.

As a young wife and mother, "What's wrong with me?" ran laps in my mind while I folded laundry, drove to drop-offs and pick-ups, and fake-smiled through another Saturday afternoon of eating cardboard pizza at yet another obligatory birthday party.

From the outside, life looked good. A beautiful family. A pretty home. Church every week. Vacations on the calendar. Target runs for the latest seasonal candle.

But inside? Going through the motions. I loved God. I believed His Word. I prayed. And I found out...

You can BELIEVE in God and still live powerless.

You can PRAY for peace and not have any.

You can WANT to exhibit the attributes of a "good" Christian but constantly fall short until you just want to stop trying.

You can be saved *and* stuck.

I felt shame over how many blessings I had, yet deep joy seemed to elude me. In all my trying, I was still frustrated and felt flat.

When I started attending a women's Bible study, it made me

mad and bitter over things that happened in my childhood. Giving grace to the people and things that had hurt me was something I wanted to do, but the study stirred up old resentments.

Bouts of depression were a struggle I tried my best to hide. Then, I was diagnosed with chronic illness, hormone imbalances, and anxiety that literally took my breath away. I was drowning...again.

When I went back to work, I had less time to dwell on the negative voices in my head. I started having career success that helped me escape and feel more valuable. I poured into women whose struggles I truly related to and stayed busy with "accomplishing" so I did not have to face what was missing.

Spiritually, I thought I knew what I needed to know. I knew God as Creator and Jesus as my Savior, but I had no idea that when I accepted Christ, the supernatural power of God came to live inside of me. He sent POWER to help, comfort, strengthen, and guide me through this crazy world.

While pursuing God, I have learned there are two ways we can ride the waves of life.

One way is to push, kick, strive, and struggle, looking for our next vacation or moment of validation.

The other is to wave our white flag of surrender.

When we wave the flag, our Lifeguard jumps in. He not only saves us from assured death, but He flips us onto our back and carries us to exactly where we are meant to be. Yes, we may still have difficulties, but now we travel with peace.

We escape treading water for a divine float, trusting the arms of our Father. No longer spinning, with our eyes fixed on heaven, we begin to move in grace upon the current.

With air in our lungs, life looks completely different. We live more relaxed and joyful. We are able to hear the birds chirp and take in the beauty all around. Fully surrendered to Him, He exchanges our weakness for His strength.

God does the heavy lifting.

Our mission changes from pushing our agenda to clinging to our Savior and His ways, carried by His power. Yes! We can have a whole new perspective and live an entirely different life in the exact same circumstances.

We often hear the encouragement, "Don't give up." But what if the real, higher invitation is not to give up? What if it is to give in? Not to apathy, but to alignment.

When you surrender to the Lord, you are not quitting. You are positioning.

So, this book is for the one who is exhausted. You feel like you are trusting God, but you are still digging in, white-knuckling through life. You thought effort would equal progress, but nothing is working, and now you are burned out.

I have been that woman. Getting my butt kicked, wave after wave, tossed around by my feelings, my weaknesses, the opinions of others, and the lies of the enemy.

Life is full of big kahunas that try to take us out, but God has other plans. Good plans. Plans to use all of your pain for good. Plans to make your dreams come true. I know this not just because I believe God's promises, but because I have lived it. I surrendered my life to Him, and everything began to change.

This is your invitation out of a powerless faith into a Spirit-drenched adventure. A life where storms refine you instead of break you. Where lies are exposed and chains fall off. Where you finally break free from the old and live with God-given authority. Where you learn to discern the voice of your enemy so you can tune him out and rise up in the truth that sets you free.

God has not missed one tear you have shed. He is here, off the deep end, offering you the ultimate life raft. And I am talking about more than getting to heaven when you leave this planet. I am talking about living the life you were made for now.

It is time to stop grasping for shifting sand like a bottom-dweller. You are God's beloved.

So, look up.

Pursue the light.

Breathe.

Take hold of the hand of the One who sets your feet on solid ground.

A great adventure awaits. It is okay to show up weak because full surrender makes room for God's greatness to take over. The tide has turned.

Are you ready? He is here to power your soul.

Jeremiah 29:11 (NIV):
"For I know the plans I have for you," declares the LORD, "plans to prosper you and not to harm you, plans to give you a hope and a future."

POWER ⚡ SOUL PLUG-IN

Reveal
What is God speaking to me through this chapter?

Reflect
Where in my life do I feel like I have been treading water instead of moving forward?

Respond
What would it look like for me to wave the white flag and let God carry what has been exhausting me?

Power Move
The next time you feel overwhelmed this week, pause before reacting.
Take one deep breath and pray,
Lord, I surrender this to You.

Pray
Jesus, I am tired of fighting waves in my own strength.
Lift me out of fear, striving, and panic.
Turn my eyes toward Your light.
Teach me to rest in Your arms and trust where You are leading me.
Breathe new life into me again.
In Jesus' name, amen.

Declaration
I do not have to drown in what God came to deliver me from.
He is my Lifeguard, my peace, and my solid ground.

2

POWER SOURCE

2 Timothy 1:6–7 (NLT):

This is why I remind you to fan into flames the spiritual gift God gave you when I laid my hands on you. For God has not given us a spirit of fear and timidity, but of power, love, and self-discipline.

Some ministries start with a pulpit. Mine started with a pitcher of milk and a bottle of chocolate syrup.

One Sunday morning, I found myself visiting a church in Southern California. The pastor came out to preach, carrying a clear glass pitcher of milk and a bottle of Hershey's syrup.

What he did next changed the way I saw my entire life.

He poured the syrup into the milk, and the glob sank to the bottom. It didn't change the milk. It just sat there. Still. Dormant.

"You see this?" he said. "This is what happens when people accept Christ but never stir up the Holy Spirit inside of them."

Then, he picked up a spoon and stirred the milk into a sweet, rich concoction—never to be the same.

Until then, I had a strong relationship with God the Father and Jesus my Savior. I studied my Bible. I had prayed many prayers. *But I didn't know or fully understand the One who was sent to live IN me.*

I received Jesus when I was nine years old. I always wanted to please God. I'd pray in my little twin bed for Him to help my parents stop fighting, help me get good grades, help my sister stop smacking her lips in her sleep, and help me not slap her if she didn't. I believed the longer I prayed, the more God would be pleased with me and would answer me. Some nights, I'd pray for hours.

I even chose Catholic catechism over Pop Warner cheer just to prove to God I loved Him.

To me, following Him meant trying harder, being good, and hoping it was enough. Only seeing a religion of works, that's what I did...work for it.

Watching the pastor stir, I recognized that I *had* the Holy Spirit but I wasn't activating His presence in my life. I had invited Him in but had not given myself over *to* Him. I was on my way to heaven but not accessing what Jesus died to give me, HERE AND NOW.

I believe this lack of knowledge is why the world is filled with worn-out saints.

Every Christian has the Holy Spirit, but the Holy Spirit doesn't have every Christian.

KNOW THE POWER BEHIND THE POWERSOUL

Before you go any further in this book, I want you to pause and get to know who I'm really talking about.

Throughout Scripture, the Holy Spirit is described in many ways. Every name He's given unveils another layer of who He is and how He operates in our lives.

WHO HE IS

The Holy Spirit is not a vague force or a religious feeling. He is God, fully divine and fully present. I want to highlight His names and where you can go in the Bible for your own deeper dive:

Holy Spirit –Luke 11:13

Spirit of God – Genesis 1:2

Spirit of the Lord – Luke 4:18

Spirit of the Lord God – Isaiah 61:1

Spirit of Christ – Romans 8:9

Spirit of Jesus – Acts 16:7

Eternal Spirit – Hebrews 9:14

He is your:

Helper – John 14:26

Advocate – John 14:16

Counselor – John 14:26

Intercessor – Romans 8:26

Spirit of Truth – John 16:13

Spirit of Grace – Hebrews 10:29

Spirit of Adoption – Romans 8:15

Spirit of Life – Romans 8:2

Spirit of Glory – 1 Peter 4:14

And when He fills you, He brings with Him:

Wisdom, Understanding, Counsel, Might, Knowledge, and the Fear of the Lord (Isaiah 11:2).

He is called:

The Promise – Acts 2:33

The Anointing – 1 John 2:27

The Seal – Ephesians 1:13

The Breath of the Almighty – Job 33:4

He is A LOT! And He is being ignored.

For those of you who just got overwhelmed by looking at all that scripture, I'll do my best to summarize:

He is one Spirit, one God with limitless power. He is not distant or abstract, and He is certainly not optional. He is extremely personal, and powerfully at work in and through the lives of those who yield to Him. I want to emphasize that last part...
for those who yield.

Yielding is choosing God's way over your impulses. To not just believe in God and Jesus but to KNOW the character and voice of God by reading what the Holy Spirit (working through men) wrote in the Bible. And then to be so close with Him that you trust Him more than you trust yourself.

You know how it is to build a relationship, right? At first, you get to know how they talk, what they think, and how they would respond. It's the great friend you send memes to because you KNOW exactly what they'd think is funny. You can hear their laugh in your head as you press send!

That's because you have taken time and energy to cultivate a close relationship with that person.

How can you know when God is talking or what He would say to your circumstances if you haven't spent enough time getting to know Him? How do you know how God would respond when you haven't learned about His character, His ways, or His goodness? Why would you trust and yield to a God when you don't know Him well and believe with every fiber of your being that He loves you beyond what you can dare imagine?

Learning to yield comes from having a close relationship with God **first.** Calling yourself a Christian or showing up at church doesn't always equate to intimacy. Just like I don't want Matt to call himself my husband and make the same reservation every Saturday night just to check a box. That isn't real love or desire.

If you're wondering why life isn't getting better even though you've accepted Christ, you must ask yourself, "Do I really know the heart of God? Am I trusting and yielding to the Holy Spirit?"

The cartoons we've all seen with the devil on one shoulder and an angel on the other is fairly accurate. There is a battle for our minds. Your flesh wants its way and pushes its weight around. The devil wants his way and will lie, steal, and cheat to get you to succumb. The Holy Spirit, on the other hand, is the only gentleman in the room, lovingly prompting you to victory. He won't scream or threaten. He won't antagonize you to do things His way. He will wait until you want His help.

Ask yourself, would the people around you call you loving? Peaceful? Joyful? Patient? Kind? Faithful? Are you someone who exhibits self-control?

When your feelings are hurt, do you run to God? Do you get quiet and pray for Him to have His way with your feelings so you don't over-react and cause more hurt?

When irritable, do you try to get away from others and pursue the presence of the Holy Spirit to be comforted and refreshed?

Are you willing to yield by giving up the last word in an argument?

Are you willing to be misunderstood, yielding, even when you feel you have the right of way?

Trust me when I say I can easily follow my feelings, causing destruction, or I can yield and take my flesh to the Holy Spirit. When I want to freak out on someone, the devil is thrilled to assist me! The Spirit of God wants to be the voice I turn to when I'm tempted. I've done both, and I'm *always* relieved when I follow the Spirit of the Lord instead of my fickle feelings. It blesses others around me when I know when to shut up too.

WE HAVE THE DIVINE HELPER, COMFORTER, AND GUIDE! THE WORD CALLS HIM OUR STANDBY...ALWAYS WAITING AND READY TO HELP US.

He is the living, breathing, wild power of God who overflows out of us when we finally take our feelings off His throne!

I'm amazed again, just writing this, because the grace of God is so amazing: first to send His Son Jesus to take our punishment THEN to send us His Spirit to empower us until we are home with Him.

Want to be like Jesus and live the life He called you to? First, you must follow Him to your own grave. Then, as you die to yourself, His Spirit rises up in you, making you a brand-new creature! HE CHANGES YOU!

Ezekiel 36:26 NLT:
And I will give you a new heart, and I will put a new spirit in you. I will take out your stony, stubborn heart and give you a tender, responsive heart.

So, back to the chocolate milk...

Here I was, 45 years old, after decades of going to church, hearing about this for the first time. I was mad that I had never understood this. All the time I spent scrapping on my own, when all along the power that rose Jesus was IN ME!?

That day changed me forever. I started praying this simple prayer each morning:

"Holy Spirit, thank you for loving and guiding me. Have Your way with me and my day. Give me Your mind, eyes, and ears. Boldly move me anyway You want."

And with this new morning prayer, things got *very* interesting, FAST...

POWER ⚡ SOUL PLUG-IN

Reveal
What is God speaking to me through this chapter?

Reflect
How has my understanding of who the Holy Spirit is been too small, distant, or incomplete?

Respond
What is one area of my life where I need to yield to the Holy Spirit instead of following my feelings, fear, or flesh?

Power Move
Before making one decision this week, pause and ask,
Holy Spirit, what is Your way here?

Pray
Holy Spirit, stir what has been dormant in me.
Help me know You more, trust Your leading, and walk in Your power today.
In Jesus' name, amen.

Declaration
The power that raised Jesus from the dead lives in me.
I will respond to Him and never live powerless again.

3

POWER OF HIS VOICE

John 10:27 (NLT):

My sheep listen to my voice,
I know them, and they follow me.

Ever buy an event ticket in advance and then totally regret it when the day arrives? Ugh...

It was a Sunday morning in May of 2017. I was dragging myself out of the door to attend a women's business event. *Who has a networker on a Sunday?* I thought to my lazy, irritated self. Months earlier, in late-night-scrolling mode, I purchased an expensive VIP ticket which included close and personal networking opportunities with some of the top entrepreneurial "boss babes." (Back then, the term *boss babe* was a compliment.) As someone deeply involved in the aesthetics industry, I saw this event as a great opportunity to bring more business to my practice. But I had completely forgotten about it *and* hadn't invited any friends or colleagues like I had originally intended. Even worse, that morning I woke up with no voice.

My voice wasn't just raspy or hoarse. It was completely gone. *Peeerrrfect*...for an all-day networker.

As I begrudgingly got ready, I started to sense that God was up to something. Heading to my car, a heavy impression from the Holy Spirit came:

I have something for you today.

It was almost vibrating in my bones, so I became much more expectant.

For the morning session, I watched "successful" women I had been following talk about building businesses, reaching goals, and shattering ceilings. They seemed powerful, polished, and strategic. But I also noticed something else: their "expert" advice didn't include a single mention of God.

Then, came the lunch break. I was seated at a table with nine beautiful women who picked at their chicken salads while chomping at the bit to mix and mingle. But I couldn't. After miming some compliments and eaves dropping on other conversations, I felt alone thinking about how many great opportunities were passing me by. So, in my frustration I did what any professional woman would do: I escaped to the restroom.

And there, in the stall, I heard the Lord: *How does it feel to not have your voice today?*

I froze. "I don't like it."

Instantly, my mind flashed back to 20 years prior at a Joyce Meyer conference. While there, I had a vision of myself speaking on stage to thousands. It sounded outrageous at the time, but deep down I believed the vision was from God and would come true.

Back to the ladies' room...

Washing my hands and processing, He showed me something that broke my heart.

There were 300 women in that room on the edge of their seats, hungry, searching, waiting for something big that would change their lives for the better. However, they needed much more than the latest social media strategy. They needed *true power* for their souls.

THEY NEEDED JESUS.

And then another word came, *Get ready to speak.*

The influencers had the microphone, the stage, and the attention to draw a large crowd...but they were leaving Him out. I could feel the grief of God. Right there in that bathroom, as I retouched my lip gloss, I made a pact with Him:

"When it's my turn to speak, Lord, I will not leave You out."

I came home, sat on the bed, and cried as I tried to explain to Matt (with no voice) what had just happened. It wasn't just emotional. I knew it was prophetic clarity. I knew that I knew that I knew:

God was activating my divine assignment. So, I started "getting ready." Not with business cards or branding packages, but by pursuing His voice. I'd start my days reading His Word and taking walks where I would pray, worship, and listen for anything He wanted to speak to my heart, gearing up for what was next.

Sometimes we get so busy chasing the things of this of this world and stuffing our schedules with to-do's. At times, I have only pursued God for what He could do for me and wasn't really listening to hear His will. He had to take my voice completely away for me to hear Him that day. And I love that He did. He wasn't going to let me miss it!

Now, I don't just talk, I take time to hear His heart, and what He reveals is incredible. He gives me strategies and ideas I would have never thought of on my own. Most of the time He softens my heart to what matters most. He reminds me to pray for others or to reach out to someone. He keeps changing me, and the more He does, the less my dreams and goals are all about me. More and more I see that everything I've ever chased is nothing compared to Him. True peace, joy, and contentment don't come with a bigger bank account or platform. Those virtues are found in His presence and in His will.

I believe He works on us until His will IS our dream.

You want life strategy? Pursue the voice of God.

READ HIS WORD

The best way is to pursue His voice in what He's already written.

Before I open the Bible or His Word in other books and resources, I invite the Holy Spirit to talk to me. I ask Him to illuminate anything He wants to show me. If it feels hard to read your Bible, get one that's easier to read. If it stills feel hard, just know the devil wants to keep your hands off it because it has the power to transform you and EVERYTHING in your life. So, tell the devil to get out of your way, in the mighty name of Jesus! Then, take action!

Hebrews 4:12 (NLT):
For the word of God is alive and powerful. It is sharper than the sharpest two-edged sword, cutting between soul and spirit, between joint and marrow. It exposes our innermost thoughts and desires.

TALK TO HIM: PRAY

If you don't know where to start, I encourage you to dissect the Lord's prayer. Jesus gave us the recipe in **Matthew 6:9–13**:

Our Father in heaven,
may your name be kept holy.
May your Kingdom come soon.
May your will be done on earth,
as it is in heaven.
Give us today the food we need,
and forgive us our sins,
as we have forgiven those who sin against us.
And don't let us yield to temptation,
but rescue us from the evil one.

Did you notice I didn't use the Bible version you've probably heard a hundred times? Because I want you to really think about it, not just recite it. Make it your own. Expand...repent, reflect.

INVITE HIM TO SPEAK TO YOU. THEN, LISTEN.

You'll read in this book about how I go on my daily walk with God because that is where I meet with Him most often. As I leave my house, I invite Him to walk and talk with me. Other times, when I'm tired, I'll ask the Holy Spirit to speak to me as I sit in silence or lay down with my eyes closed. Many times, as I listen to worship music and sing praises, the Lord speaks to my heart. Maybe this is all old news to you, but a reminder never hurts!

I just know that when we want to meet with God, He wants to meet with us. And when we are determined to hear Him, He speaks.

The more you pursue His voice, the more He will speak to you.

POWER ⚡ SOUL PLUG-IN

Reveal
What is God speaking to me through this chapter?

Reflect
What voices have been shaping my thoughts, decisions, or desires more than the voice of God?

Respond
What is one practical way I can make more room this week to hear God through His Word, prayer, worship, or quiet time?

Power Move
Set aside ten uninterrupted minutes this week to meet with God.
Ask one question, then listen.

Pray
Lord, quiet every competing voice around me and within me.
Open my ears to hear You, and give me the courage to follow what You say.
In Jesus' name, amen.

Declaration
I am not confused, distracted, or without direction.
I know His voice, and I am learning to follow His lead.

4

POWER TO JUMP

Joshua 1:9 (NLT):

This is my command—be strong and courageous! Do not be afraid or discouraged. For the Lord your God is with you wherever you go.

Have you ever stood on the edge of something you knew God was calling you into but still hesitated? That's where trust begins.

We've all seen it: a little kid standing at the edge of a pool, wanting so badly to jump into the fun and swim, but instead he stands frozen in fear. Frozen.

His dad calls to him from the water with arms stretched wide. "Jump, son! I've got you!"

The boy knows his dad is good and won't let him drown. But it's still not enough. He bites his nails. Hesitates. Thinks. Waits. Stalls. And while he's waiting, he's missing out.

Finally, miserable in his current state, he jumps! But not to his father. He jumps sideways—toward the edge of the pool—grabbing for the wall, almost cracking his head. His little body lands with a splash and a scrape. Yes, he made it into the water, but he's not free.

That's what my "obedience" looked like when God first told me to leave my career.

About nine months after the Lord whispered *Get ready to speak*, I was going through my morning routine—coffee, couch, and Bible—before jumping up to spackle myself together for another day at work when I heard:

Quit your job, today.

I froze. I knew this day would come but, *today?* So, like a responsible adult, I ignored it and went to work.

Late that afternoon, both surgeons I worked for were in the office at the same time, which rarely happened. They usually alternated days. But that day, they both needed to meet with me to talk about insurance changes. That's when the Holy Spirit whispered again:

I told you to quit—today.

I felt it in my bones. This wasn't coincidence; it was a divine setup. So, instead of giving them time to launch into a conversation about insurance plans, I started to cry and told them I was giving notice.

One looked at me with understanding and joy. The other raised a brow in disbelief. Each of their faces mirrored my own mixed emotions as I explained how God had been stirring something in me for months and I had to obey. They were shocked but kind. Then, they offered me a reduced role so I could keep a small paycheck and I took it.

At the time, it felt like wisdom...to ease out...not to jump. Looking back, it was compromise dressed as safety. I had jumped sideways, clinging to my own idea of what would be best.

I had built a beautiful career in medical aesthetics over the course of nearly two decades. Many of my clients had become dear friends because I loved helping them feel beautiful and confident. It was my art form, and I was scared to fully let it go. Especially because I had worked so hard to build my career to this level

Walking away meant more than losing a good job. I'd be leaving real money, bonuses, luxurious skincare perks, and the pride of knowing I could always provide for myself. Even though I'm married, that felt *very* good.

I came from humble beginnings. When my parents divorced at 14, money was especially tight, so I lied about my age to get a job at a local pizza joint. I was extremely motivated by the idea of going to high school without new clothes and burdening my mom more than she already was. I was never afraid to work hard for a better life. After my first marriage failed, I became a single mom with a young toddler, attending aesthetic school during the day and waiting tables at night. All of that so I could one day have an awesome career like this one.

The moment I accepted the smaller role, everything at work started to fall apart.

My hands, once steady in every treatment, began to shake. The anointing was gone. Work relationships that once energized and brightened my day felt strained. The atmosphere felt heavy, and I no longer felt joy being there. Now, I knew I was working without God's blessing, and that began to scare me more than leaving.

I stayed when I wasn't supposed to, and my last days at the practice I once loved were filled with sadness and confusion. *And all that misery was the grace of God.* He knew I *had to* hate hanging on in order to let go.

And when I did, relief came over me and my joy returned almost immediately. I knew God had a great plan and I was determined not to miss it.

It's not enough to believe in God. Even Satan and his minions *believe* in God. Real victory is found in *following* Him in obedience because you know His plans will always trump yours. The faster you learn to jump when Father says *jump*, the better your life will be and the less suffering you'll have and create for others.

Trust isn't blind. It's built on knowing the character of the One calling you forward. The closer your relationship is with God, the more you'll see His faithfulness and the more natural and easier this becomes.

WHEN OBEDIENCE FEELS LIKE MADNESS

Like quitting my job, sometimes obedience won't make sense to anyone around you. Sometimes it won't even make sense to you! It can look like crazy and feel risky. But if God is asking you to, He isn't asking for your logic. He's asking you to trust.

If you're clinging to a situation that used to be good, but deep down, you know it's over stop calling it loyalty. Stop calling it wisdom. Call it what it is: *fear*. Fearing the unknown, change, and transition will keep you stuck. God allows discomfort to protect your destiny. If He's nudging you to jump and you're still clinging to the edge, you're not in faith. You're agreeing with the devil in fear.

Stop praying for God to help you in a situation He has already asked you to leave. Sound scary? Count the cost. You want to miss the awesome life He has for you because you won't leave the baby pool? When God invites you to release what feels safe, familiar, and comfortable, He's leading you into everything He always knew you were created for!

This trust intersection is where you go from a believer to a true follower of Christ.

Matthew 16:24 (NLT):
Then Jesus said to his disciples, "If any of you wants to be my follower, you must give up your own way, take up your cross and follow me."

In Scripture, Matthew wasn't broke or desperate. He had a prosperous job, one that guaranteed income and security in the world's eyes. As a tax collector, people may have hated him, but they couldn't deny he had position and stability. Then, Jesus walked by, and with one request, "Follow Me," Matthew was confronted with the truth the world never tells you: ***safe doesn't mean purposeful.*** The moment Christ called him, he left his old life without hesitation and stepped into a destiny no paycheck could ever buy.

There was no guarantee of safety or success, but Matthew recognized something divine.

If you have been sensing a Holy Spirit pull, don't keep asking for more confirmation. Ask for courage.

Whatever He is nudging you to do, do it. Make the call. Send the email. Submit the resignation. Take the class. Book the ticket. Close the door.

Jump.

The water of destiny is deep, but the Father is waiting. And He's never failed. Ever.

Hebrews 11:6 (NLT):

And it is impossible to please God without faith. Anyone who wants to come to him must believe that God exists and that he rewards those who sincerely seek him.

POWER ⚡ SOUL PLUG-IN

Reveal
What is God speaking to me through this chapter?

Reflect
Where in my life am I still clinging to the edge of what feels safe instead of trusting God enough to jump?

Respond
What step of obedience have I delayed because fear, comfort, or logic has been louder than faith?

Power Move
Take one bold action this week toward what God has already been nudging you to do.
Make the call, send the email, start the process, or close the door.

Pray
Father, give me courage to trust You beyond what feels safe.
Help me release the edge and follow where You are leading me.
In Jesus' name, amen.

Declaration
I do not have to fear the unknown when God is calling me forward.
The One asking me to jump is faithful to catch me.

5

POWER OF THE CAVE

Hebrews 11:1:

Now faith is confidence in what we hope for and assurance about what we do not see.

Fast forward one year....

There I was on my hands and knees, in the middle of the day, scrubbing a spot on my bedroom carpet. No job, platform, or plan.

I wasn't speaking anywhere or preaching. I was just a woman trying to wrap my head around a new calling, wondering how anyone would take me seriously as a preacher when just last year I was promoting lip filler.

I knew I had to fill my mind with truth or I'd drown in doubt. The imposter syndrome was loud. During this time, leadership podcasts became my lifeline, filling my mind with stories of people who answered the call on their lives and were willing to be terrible at something new before ever becoming any good.

Was I willing to go through the uncomfortable and embarrassing season of trial and error? Could I post what God put on my heart, even if I was misunderstood or judged?

Yes.

I decided I would be willing, and that was a turning point for me. If God is truly first in my life, then my reputation with people can't be. I had to be determined to walk in the identity He gave me, even if I felt like a dork at first. So many Christians sing songs of surrender or pray, "Lord, send me," but when it gets uncomfortable, they back down.

At first, I expected it to happen fast. Like, "Ta-da! Doors open!" I thought I'd leave my career and BOOM! Divine acceleration! I had answered the call, right? Instead, I found myself in what felt like a long, dark hallway. The kind you walk through slowly, with your hands on the walls, feeling your way forward. I like to call this season of my life, the cave.

Romans 8:28 (NLT):
And we know that God causes everything to work together for the good of those who love God and are called according to his purpose for them.

Verses like this one were the lifelines I held onto, and even though I couldn't see where I was going, I kept moving anyway. I clung to promises like a blindfolded traveler feeling for the next step, trusting His Word even when I couldn't see where I was going. I wrestled with frustration and the silence. Some days were a struggle, but I refused to lose faith.

Scrubbing that carpet, tears brimming in my eyes, I cried out, "God, I don't know what else to do. Please send help."

Help came. Not in a beam of light through my bedroom ceiling, but in practical, divine connections that started showing up like bricks illuminating a new path.

JESUS IN THE WILDERNESS

Before I share what happened next, let me remind you that even Jesus had a hidden season. After He was baptized and publicly affirmed as God's Son, He didn't go straight to healing or preaching.

Luke 4:1–2:
Jesus, full of the Holy Spirit ... was led by the Spirit in the wilderness for forty days ... being tempted by the devil.

For 40 days He fasted in isolation. And when He was extremely tired and hungry, the enemy tested Him, taunting Him to prove Himself when He didn't have to.

The devil will tempt you too. Just like the enemy tried to get Jesus to perform, the enemy will try to get you to perform for the approval of others and seek validation.

The enemy will also tempt you to follow your flesh, giving in to the cravings of shopping, food, sex, drinking, drugs, affirmations, and every other distraction under the sun. He wants you to stay comfortable, wasting time, scrolling...because **comfort will kill your calling.**

If that doesn't work, he'll promise you power or a short cut if you compromise.

But Jesus stood His ground against the enemy and emerged from that season *in power* (Luke 4:14), ready to walk in His full authority.

The wilderness was His preparation. If Jesus needed a season of isolation before stepping into His divine calling, why do *we* think we can bypass it?

Like I said, I finally asked God to help me, and doors started to open in that dark hallway. Doors to classrooms...

THE COACHING CERTIFICATION

I discovered a Christian coaching program through Freedom Academy in Southern California. After praying with and advising women for years, I sensed God asking me to step all the way in and become better equipped.

Their three-day course wasn't just about earning my certification or learning how to be a better coach. It was about inviting Jesus to heal me anywhere I needed it first.

And that's exactly what I needed. I didn't realize how much pain I had shoved down while functioning as a "high-capacity woman." While experiencing personal breakthroughs, the program gave me language, clarity, and a deeper anointing to help others. I left the course understanding that no matter how much I want to help someone, I AM NOT THE SAVIOR and that creating space for others to experience Jesus themselves was my ultimate goal.

THE SPEAKING COURSE

Soon after, I found a beautiful Christian couple online: David and Angelike Norrie. I knew it in my gut that these entrepreneurial rockstars were supposed to be my friends. They just didn't know it yet!

On social media, I had submitted a video audition for a women's speaking event, and David happened to see it. He offered me a spot in his professional, public speaking course. No one was asking me to speak yet, but I knew joining this was part of my preparation.

I showed up as the oldest and most anxious student in the room. For the first couple of Zoom classes, my voice wavered with nerves, causing me to dread showing up. But I did. When I finished that course, I had a toolkit, a testimony, and a lot more confidence to speak publicly.

THE HEALING

During this time, I went to a local event to hear a well-known motivational speaker. I wasn't sure if he was a "manifest your dream life" kind of guy or someone God was using, and I wanted to find out.

An old knee injury had me in chronic pain. It wasn't fixable, at least that's what the doctors said. "Just manage it," they told me.

Limping up the Spanish style steps to the conference room, I could hear worship music playing, and my guard went down. The presence of the Holy Spirit was thick. The speaker had such a great style. He was anointed but relatable, and I loved it. Toward the end of the evening, he started to call people to the front of the room who needed healing. My eyes popped when I watched a woman with knotted, arthritic hands stretch out her healed fingers right in front of me. I was blown away. It was like the Book of Acts.

In such awe, I hadn't even considered asking for help for myself when the preacher, leaving the platform, walked by, reached down, looked me in the eyes, and quickly grabbed my hands in a shake goodbye. No prayer or anything dramatic. Just a two-second moment.

As I exited down the bumpy, tile stairs, I waited for the familiar flinch of knee pain, but it didn't come. *Maybe I'm on a Holy Spirit high, and that's why I'm not in pain, I thought.* But the next morning, as I stood in the shower, shaving my legs, it hit me.

I am standing on that leg with all of my weight! Something I hadn't done in years. I cried in amazement, blessed by another miracle. Looking back, I can see what I couldn't see then. When I moved forward in faith, the Lord moved too.

God reveals more of Himself to us in the secret place. You may not see the light yet, but the cave is holy ground.

It's where He forms your character, stretches your faith, and roots your identity deeper in Him. The space between the *yes* and the *what's next* is sacred, and honestly, it's the foundation for everything God is going to use you to build. *This is not a time of punishment; it's an awesome privilege where God wants you all to Himself.* This season is vital to your calling, and God is good to hide you while He refines you.

He wants to walk this out *with* you, at His pace, because each step is essential to who you will become. The person He has called will not be the same person who fulfills it. He takes us through a process, but that doesn't mean we are idle. By preparing for the call on our life, we express faith in God and the future us.

Maybe you think nothing is moving because you aren't.

Time in the cave isn't wasted. God is interested in who you're becoming because who you are will overflow into everything you do. The more you become like Christ, the more you will impact the world like He does.

Surrender the timeline. Release every expectation of how you thought this would go. Thank Him for divine delays, hidden doors, and quiet preparation. Ask Him to root you deeply in His voice and to show you how to use what you already carry. Ask Him to help you walk this path with faith, not fear. And when the time comes, He will open doors only He can open.

Proverbs 3:5–6:
Trust in the Lord with all your heart;
do not depend on your own understanding.
Seek His will in all you do,
and He will show you which path to take.

POWER ⚡ SOUL PLUG-IN

Reveal
What is God speaking to me through this chapter?

Reflect
How might God be using this hidden or uncertain season to prepare me for what is ahead?

Respond
What expectation, timeline, or need for visible progress do I need to surrender so I can embrace this season well?

Power Move
Choose one way to prepare this week instead of waiting frustrated.
Learn, practice, heal, pray, study, or build what is already in your hand.

Pray
Lord, help me trust You in seasons I do not understand.
Refine my heart and prepare me for what is ahead.
In Jesus' name, amen.

Declaration
This season is holy where I am being set apart.
God is forming me in a profound way to prepare me for the doors ahead.

6

POWER OF THE CROWN

1 Peter 2:9:

You are a chosen people, a royal priesthood...

"Who do you think you are?"

When I first started writing this book, I had a publisher who assigned me a "Christian" ghostwriter to help get me started. His first encouraging words to me were, "Why would anyone want to read your story? You aren't Oprah."

After months of taking his advice, I was confused, disoriented, and paralyzed. The devil was using him to try and discourage me, and it was working. Finally, he admitted he didn't believe in the whole Bible and tried to turn what you're about to read into a ten-page children's book. The one I was trusting as the "expert" was trying to get me to abandon my God-given ideas and assignment. This was just the first of many attacks against this book. Before I could even start, this book had enemies.

Then, my fears of putting something permanent out into the world—something flawed to be judged—tried to sabotage me. It took me years to get over my people-pleasing ways and stop needing approval, and this experience was putting my confidence to the test.

BUT GOD.

Many years prior, the Lord powerfully revealed to me my true identity. And in these moments of doubt, I decided to cling to that moment instead of the lies of the enemy.

Flashback to 2008...

The real estate market crashed. Like so many others, our family felt the ripple effect. My husband Matt had to leave real estate and take a corporate job just to keep us afloat. Our girls were older, more independent, and I knew it was time for me to return to work.

Even though I was a licensed aesthetician, I didn't have time to rebuild my business. So, for fast cash I did something that felt like survival and surrender in the same breath: I got a job waiting tables at the coolest little restaurant in town. But I didn't feel cool. Nope, not at all.

On one of my first mornings, I was prepping the restaurant when one of my coworkers, (a guy young enough to be my son) looked straight at me and said, "What's on your face?!"

I ran to the restroom to find blood running down my chin from a spot on my lip, like something out of a vampire movie. Mortified, I wiped it away, realizing my body was manifesting the stress of all I was carrying. A cold sore? I'd never had a cold sore before. I didn't even know what it was. Great. Now I'm the old lady who has herpes on the team. I wanted to run out the back door.

The next day, as I was driving back to work in a spirit of dread. I didn't want to go. My prayers turned into bargaining with God. "Do I really have to do this? Is this where I'm supposed to be? Should I just turn around?"

That's when I heard the Holy Spirit speak, gentle but firm, to my heart:

Who am I?

I paused. "You're the King."

If I'm the King and you're My daughter, what does that make you?

Deep breath…"A princess."

But the label princess never sat naturally with me. As a little girl, I was a blonde, daydreamer who was often labeled as an airhead. I didn't like or want the bubblegum-pink, tiara-wearing image. Princesses were dumb and fragile. I was none of that. (For years I wouldn't even wear pink.)

But then God asked me to think of a real-life princess. The only one who came to mind was Princess Kate. And the Lord said:

Princess Kate knows exactly who she is. She walks in her earthly title with authority. Without arrogance, she carries the dignity of her position in the kingdom she represents. She doesn't apologize for it or shrink back. She moves in the fullness of it, in strength and grace. If you knew who you were as My daughter in My Kingdom, you'd walk differently, talk differently and change the atmosphere just be being in the room.

As I sat there, letting that sink in, something shifted in me.

The enemy had been trying to reduce me into insecurity, comparison, and shame. But God was calling me out of that fog and into the truth of who I *really* am: ROYALTY.

I wiped my tears, squared my shoulders, and drove to work with a different attitude.

As I checked in that morning, the manager—who knew nothing about my conversation with God—looked at me and said with a smile, “Good morning, PRINCESS!”

I nearly fell over!

From that day, I’ve collected crowns as a reminder of truth and identity. I like to give them away to women and remind them who they are in the eyes of God. And anytime someone is messing with my confidence...I remember whose I am.

The truth is, I never wanted to be Oprah or anyone else. Nor do I have to be to make an impact. And I know the only way this book would be a failure is if I gave up on it, out of the fear of man.

When you aren’t solid in your identity as a beloved daughter of the King, the enemy is more than happy to fit you with his counterfeit crown of insecurity.

Your identity isn’t in what you do, how you look, or how others see you. It’s not rooted in titles, money, or status.

Your identity is rooted in Jesus alone.

Not because you earned it, but because God put such a high value on you that He sent His one and only beloved Son Jesus Christ to shed His priceless blood for YOU.

1 Peter 1:18–19 (NLT):
For you know that God paid a ransom to save you from the empty life you inherited from your ancestors... It was not paid with mere gold or silver... It was the precious blood of Christ, the sinless, spotless Lamb of God.

Maybe you’ve been walking into rooms without the holy confidence Jesus died to give you. Maybe you’ve always felt like "too much" or "not enough." Maybe you're in a situation today that's not ideal, and you're questioning yourself and God's plan because you feel judged and insignificant.

I'm here to tell you that ***any*** voice that slithers up, contradicting God, comes from one place: THE PIT OF HELL.

I ended up having a lot of fun at that restaurant job. I got in great shape, met new friends (who I ministered to), and relieved some financial stress for my family.

I, "Princess Brandie," learned to KNOW my worth with an empty bank account, a scab on my lip, slinging thin-crust pizzas.

Bottom line: there will always be something to make you feel bad about yourself unless you ***choose*** to believe in your God-given identity. Only then will you walk as His daughter or stand like His son.

Romans 8:16–17:
The Spirit Himself testifies with our spirit that we are God's children. Now if we are children, then we are heirs...

POWER ⚡ SOUL PLUG-IN

Reveal
What is God speaking to me through this chapter?

Reflect
Where have I been wearing a counterfeit crown of insecurity, comparison, shame, or the need for approval?

Respond
What would change in the way I walk, speak, or show up if I fully believed I am God's beloved child?

Power Move
Notice one moment this week when insecurity tries to shrink you.
Pause, reject the lie, and choose to respond from your true identity instead.

Pray
Father, remove every false label I have carried.
Teach me to see myself through Your eyes and live from the identity You gave me.
In Jesus' name, amen.

Declaration
Because I belong to the Most High King, I will walk in holy confidence.

7

POWER HUG

John 16:13 (NLT):

When the Spirit of truth comes, he will guide you into all truth.

When I was working as an aesthetician in a plastic surgeon's office, many of our patients were breast cancer survivors. One of my roles was to perform areola tattooing after reconstruction, and it was a privilege to help restore a sense of wholeness to women who had been through so much.

One afternoon, I was asked to consult with a woman experiencing skincare issues from her cancer treatments. I'll call her Linda.

Before I went into the room, my colleague quietly let me know that Linda and her sister had just been told she needed a mastectomy. They were both visibly distraught, so I was advised to keep the consultation short and sweet so they could go grieve in private.

Carrying products in my hands, I stepped into the room ready to help. I stayed in professional mode at first, explaining options and moving efficiently, until her phone rang and everything shifted.

Her ringtone was a Christian worship song I recognized, and in that moment, I felt the Holy Spirit tug on my heart. I paused, set the products aside, and looked her in the eyes.

"I want you both to know something," I said softly. "I'm one of the last people who sees our patients before they leave here whole, restored, beautiful, and healed. I know you're just beginning this journey, and it's scary. But I heard your ringtone, and I want you to know, you worship the same God I do. He's with you. He hasn't left you. He will walk with you through every part of this."

We both began to cry and stood up to embrace.

But when I went to release her, I couldn't. My arms wouldn't move. An invisible force was holding me there, keeping me wrapped around her longer than I would have chosen on my own.

With a nervous laugh, I said, "I'm sorry...I think I'm supposed to hug you longer, because I can't let you go."

We laughed through tears, and after what felt like the longest hug ever, I was finally able to let go and send them on their way.

The next day, Linda called. She told me that right after she left my office, her phone rang again. It was her husband. He asked why she hadn't been answering, and she explained she had been in a consultation.

Then he told her, "I felt terrible for not being with you today, so I kept praying that God would hug you for me."

Over the phone, we wept again. I saw what could happen when I made room for Him to move, and I knew I would never be the same. I wanted my life to look like this every day.

A few days later, she returned with her sister and mother to give me a necklace. She called me an angel and kept thanking me.

But I knew the truth. It wasn't me. I had simply made myself available.

The love that met her in that room was God's. In one of the most vulnerable moments of her life, He made Himself known to her in a way that was deeply personal and impossible to dismiss.

What looked like an interruption became a divine appointment. A simple hug became an answer to prayer. God is so present and personal. He wants to move in the details of our lives.

I've thought about that day many times and wondered what would have happened if I had "stirred the Spirit" but ignored the nudge, stayed efficient, and finished the consultation without ever pausing. I would have done my job well, but I would have missed the miracle.

Everything God speaks to us is meant to be lived out, not just learned. Scripture calls us not to be hearers only, but doers of the Word.

James 1:22 (NLT):
But don't just listen to God's word. You must do what it says. Otherwise, you are only fooling yourselves.

The more we do what we learn and follow His lead, the more we experience fantastic moments like this.

As a Christian, He lives in you, but He will not force His way. He responds to invitation. So, prepare your heart each morning to be used by God by inviting the Holy Spirit to your conversations, interruptions and schedule.

And when you make yourself available, you may find that God wants to move through you in ways that are far more powerful and unexpected than you ever imagined.

POWER ⚡ SOUL PLUG-IN

Reveal
What is God speaking to me through this chapter?

Reflect
Where might I be moving too quickly, staying guarded, or staying efficient in moments where God wants to love someone through me?

Respond
How can I become more available to the Holy Spirit in my daily conversations, interruptions, and ordinary moments?

Power Move
Before you begin your day this week, pray a simple prayer:
Holy Spirit, make me available to love someone the way You want to today.

Pray
Lord, open my eyes to the people around me and soften my heart to Your nudges.
Use my ordinary moments for Your extraordinary love.
In Jesus' name, amen.

Declaration
I will not miss divine appointments by rushing past them.
God can move through my willingness, compassion, and obedience.

8

POWER OF PRAISE

Psalm 103:2:

Let all that I am praise the LORD; may I never forget the good things he does for me.

Shortly after the women's event where God told me to *get ready*, someone very dear to me went to heaven. This was unexpected and devastating. I could feel my heart breaking in my chest. I traveled to be with her grieving mother and saw firsthand how the grief had broken her spirit. Usually, she was the most joyful person, full of faith. But now her spark was gone, and my heart broke even more.

Trying to be strong for her, I held it together until I couldn't. So, I did what I always do when I need to hear from God: I took a walk. As I walked and prayed, I told Him I wasn't going back to the house until I heard from Him. I *needed* something. I *needed* Him to tell me why this happened. I *needed* to take some encouragement back with me.

I walked and walked. Nothing.

The sun started to set over the ocean. I was in the most beautiful place, but the beauty was lost on me because my soul was so heavy with pain.

I was far away from the house at this point, and I said to the Lord again, "I'm not going back until You speak to me." (He said knock and the door will be opened...am I right?!)

Then, I heard the Spirit:

Be more grateful.

Huh?

I knew this was not my thought. It was Him. So, for nearly an hour, I spoke aloud everything I was grateful for and praised God. The other walkers passing by looked at me like I was nuts, but I didn't care. I needed relief.

My anger and despair lifted as gratitude rose. I had been so focused on what was going wrong that I'd lost sight of everything that was going right. After three days of dwelling on loss, I was in a pit. But when I took my focus off my sadness and looked up toward Him, He reached down and lifted me out.

Isaiah 61:3:
To all who mourn in Israel,
he will give a crown of beauty for ashes,
a joyous blessing instead of mourning,
festive praise instead of despair.
In their righteousness, they will be like great oaks
that the Lord has planted for his own glory.

What a powerful verse. When we mourn, He gives us a garment of praise, *but we must put it on*. We must act against despair. We take off the garment of heaviness by putting on the garment of praise.

It's a decision.

Gratitude, in all circumstances, helps us remember how good God is *even when* experiencing pain. Praising Him when it's hard and we don't feel like it gives us the peace and strength we desperately need. There is tremendous *power* in a sacrifice of praise; I believe that's why it's so hard to do.

On that same trip, my friend's mother and I were stuck in holiday traffic, driving through a dark desert, when a different friend reached out to us. She said, "I asked God to send me a song that would encourage you both. "I asked God for the perfect song so the first one on the radio is the one I'll send." But when she first turned on the radio all she heard was white noise. (In a major city, that just doesn't happen.) Then, through the static, a song began to play. She recorded some of it with her phone and sent it to me. We listened as its lyrics described how **God is with us in the dark and in the desert.**

We laughed as tears streamed down our faces. This was our first burst of joy in days.

I could never find the song she sent again. It was a gift from God for that exact moment. A gift just for us. He hadn't left us alone in our heartache, He was there to light up our darkness.

Psalm 34:17–19 NLT:
The LORD hears his people when they call to him for help.
He rescues them from all their troubles.
The LORD is close to the brokenhearted;
he rescues those whose spirits are crushed.
The righteous person faces many troubles,
but the LORD comes to the rescue each time.

A few weeks later, I experienced another form of grief. Our beloved family dog Herbie had to be put down after 16 wonderful years. I couldn't bear to go with my husband and daughter to the vet for his last moments, so instead, I went to

Home Depot to buy cleaning supplies. I needed the distraction, and the last few weeks of Herbie's life made for messy floors.

New mop in hand, I went to wipe away his paw prints, but I couldn't do it. His empty bowl brought a wave of grief that I had tried not to feel. I sat down in his mess and cried. And there, God spoke to my heart again:

Look at how much you love this dog. An animal that never even said a word to you, and yet you love him so much you want to sit in his filth. How much more do you think I'm willing to sit with you in yours?

God doesn't just draw near to us when we are clean and ready. He loves us enough to sit with us in our darkest moments and even in the places of our life where we have made a big mess. And His Word promises us that when we decide to look to Him and cling to Him instead of our losses and messes of life, He will carry us through. God is with you in your darkest pain, so take it all to Him. Nothing you're experiencing is too big for Him. He loves you deeply and wants to relieve you.

You are never alone.
Even in grief, God walks with you.
Even in anger, He listens.
Even in the dark, He shines.
Gratitude lifts your heaviness.
Praise Him with your tears, and He will power your soul.

Psalm 147:3 (NLT):
He heals the brokenhearted and bandages their wounds.

God doesn't always change our circumstances. But remember, as we draw close to Him, He changes us. And when we change, everything changes.

POWER SOUL PLUG-IN

Reveal
What is God speaking to me through this chapter?

Reflect
Where have grief, disappointment, or heaviness caused me to lose sight of God's goodness?

Respond
What can I thank God for today, even in the middle of what feels hard?

Power Move
Take a gratitude walk or set aside 30 minutes to speak aloud every blessing, big or small.
Put praise music in your ears until praise starts to come out of your mouth.
Sing to the Lord.

Pray
Lord, meet me in my pain and lift the heaviness from my soul.
Help me remember Your goodness and praise You in every season.
In Jesus' name, amen.

Declaration
Heaviness will not have the final word over me.
As I praise God, peace, strength, and hope rise again.

9

POWER OF EXPECTATION

Proverbs 13:12 (NLT):

Hope deferred makes the heart sick,
but a dream fulfilled is a tree of life.

There is a different kind of grief that can be detrimental to your faith and your future: disappointment. The kind that causes deep discouragement, taking root in your soul. Convincing you that's it's better to prepare for the worst than to expect the best.

When something miserable drags on long enough, people are tempted to stop expecting God. So, the enemy uses disappointment to wear down and extinguish our hope. If he can convince a believer that nothing will change, he can slowly get them to stop praying, stop believing, and stop reaching for God at all. A heart that has stopped expecting anything eventually settles into hopelessness.

Jesus spoke these words to His disciples shortly before His arrest and crucifixion:

John 16:33 (NLT):
I have told you all this so that you may have peace in me. Here on earth you will have many trials and sorrows. But take heart, because I have overcome the world.

He wasn't trying to soften reality or offer empty comfort. He knew exactly what was coming and wanted them to understand something important before He left them. Life in this world will be very hard at times. There will be seasons of confusion, pressure, and disappointment. Following Him would not remove these things.

But He did not stop with a warning. He followed it with a command that changes how a believer is meant to live in the middle of trouble:

Take heart.

In Jesus' language, Aramaic, He was saying much more than what the English translation gives us. He was saying, BE STRONG. BE COURAGEOUS. STAND FIRM.

The phrase Jesus used carries the idea of refusing to let fear and discouragement take over your heart when pressure comes.

Yes, said trials and sorrows will come, but He gave us a way to live when they do. Defeat is not meant to define the life of someone who belongs to God.

One of my favorite scriptures reminds us why:

Romans 8:28 (NLT):
And we know that God causes everything to work together for the good of those who love God and are called according to his purpose for them.

This promise always changes the way I face difficulty. Trouble no longer has the final word. God is capable of taking even the things that feel painful or unfair and weaving them into something good...for those who love Him.

Because of His promise, we are able to live with a kind of expectation that the world doesn't understand.

Expectation does not mean manifesting the future through a positive outlook. And it doesn't mean pretending problems don't exist. Expectation grows out of trust in God's love for us and His character.

I recently heard a story on a podcast that illustrates how expectation shapes the way we live. A woman had her heart broken when her boyfriend broke up with her. When she eventually met someone new that she was excited about, the fear of being hurt again began to shape how she showed up in the relationship. She became anxious, guarded, and suspicious. Instead of enjoying what was unfolding, she constantly prepared herself for the moment things would fall apart. When was the other shoe going to drop?

You guessed it...he broke up with her too.

But the man didn't reject the real her. He had only experienced the paranoid version. The one already expecting to be let down.

Her disappointment took root and morphed into fear. And fear has a way of making people brace for loss before anything has even happened.

Fear pulls hell up into your life. Faith pulls heaven down.

I love how the Bible shows us people who experienced deep suffering and still chose to move toward God instead of away from Him. One of the clearest examples is the woman who had been bleeding for twelve years.

Twelve years is a very long time to live with a chronic health problem. During those years she had spent everything she had trying to find help. According to Scripture, the treatments she pursued didn't work. On top of her physical suffering, her condition made her ceremonially unclean. That meant she lived on the outskirts of society...alone and completely shunned.

Can you imagine?

By the time she heard that Jesus, the Messiah, was passing through town, she had already experienced many years of disappointment. Most people in her situation would have given up hope long before.

Yet when word spread that Jesus was coming, something in her refused to surrender to despair. She became determined to see Jesus.

Scripture tells us she said to herself, "If I can just touch His robe, I will be healed."

Those words reveal her expectation!

She did not know exactly how a miracle would unfold or if Jesus would even notice her in the crowd. But she believed if she could just get close enough to Him, something would change. So, she *took heart* and pushed through the crowd.

When she touched the edge of His robe, Jesus stopped in the middle of everyone and spoke to her with love. "Daughter," He said, "go in peace, your faith has healed you."

After twelve years of disappointment...healing came!

She was healed by the faith that moved her toward Jesus when disappointment could have kept her away.

The enemy often works through the past. He reminds you of what happened last time, the door that closed, the prayer that seemed unanswered, the situation that didn't turn out the way you hoped. Because if he can't keep you out of heaven, his goal is to shrink you down into a pitiful, heart-sick "believer", living without joy, peace and strength. Holy Spirit Power AND hopelessness are not compatible.

The Bible promises that strength returns to people who keep placing their confidence in God rather than in their circumstances:

Isaiah 40:31 (NLT):
But those who trust in the Lord will find new strength.
They will soar high on wings like eagles.
They will run and not grow weary.
They will walk and not faint.

Faith remembers who God is.

David stood in front of Goliath with nothing more than a sling and a stone because he was convinced that the battle belonged to the Lord. Joshua and Caleb looked at the same giants everyone else saw in the Promised Land, but their expectation was in God's promise more than the size of the obstacle.

Are you tired of waiting for your miracle? Jesus sees you and He has an answer!

BE STRONG! BE COURAGEOUS! STAND FIRM!

REFUSE TO BOW TO FEAR! KEEP YOUR FAITH! PURSUE THE LORD, EVEN IN PAIN! LIFT YOUR EYES! KEEP EXPECTING GOD!

Because the One who overcame the world is STILL at work in the middle of your story.

Always, TAKE HEART!

POWER ⚡ SOUL PLUG-IN

Reveal
What is God speaking to me through this chapter?

Reflect
Where has disappointment tried to lower my expectations, weaken my faith, or convince me to stop hoping?

Respond
What promise, prayer, or area of my life do I need to bring back under hopeful expectation with God?

Power Move
Take heart today.
Write down what you are believing God for, then pray over it with faith instead of fear.
Choose to *expect* His goodness again.

Pray
Lord, heal every place disappointment has made my heart weary.
Restore my hope, strengthen my faith, and teach me to expect You again.
In Jesus' name, amen.

Declaration
My past disappointments do not define my future.
God is still working, still faithful, and still able to do the impossible.

10

POWER IN WEAKNESS

Matthew 11:28:

Come to me, all you who are weary and burdened, and I will give you rest.

I couldn't breathe.

It felt like a walnut was stuck in my throat. My chest felt constricted and my heart started pounding uncontrollably.

My daughters were out in the living room and I didn't want to scare them. So, I quietly shut my bedroom door, sat on the edge of my bed, and googled my symptoms. "Panic attack."

Of course, I had been stressed many times before. I lived most of my life in fight or flight. In the fifth grade I developed a stomach ulcer from stress and worry, but this...this was different. My mind was spinning, and no matter how much I tried to calm down, my body wouldn't listen.

It happened as I was packing for a long weekend with my extended family. Anyone else feel anxious when it's time to be in inescapable quarters with ten other people who all have their own agendas and unresolved issues?

Not knowing what else to do, I crawled onto my bed on my knees and curled over, putting my head in my hands and started to pray.

"Help me, Lord. Help me, Lord. Help me, Lord..."

That's when He gave me a vision.

I saw a baby in the middle of a full-blown tantrum. All tensed up, not able to breathe with tears streaming down its bright red face, so overcome with emotion that she was completely inconsolable. Then, from sheer exhaustion...the baby finally melted into her mother's arms, receiving the comfort that had been there all along. Safe and soothed.

I was that baby...trying so hard to power through my overwhelm that my body went into a full-blown fit. If I wasn't going to call 911, I needed a miracle.

With no strength left to resist, I stopped trying. I focused on the presence of God and exhaled everything I'd been holding in. In my weakness, I collapsed into the arms of my Father. As He held me in His presence, His peace started to replace my panic. Exhale...

Like the cold sweat that comes after throwing up, it wiped me out, but I felt cleansed. Laying there in relief that the worst had passed, the Holy Spirit whispered something:

Think of someone you really love. (I immediately thought of my daughters.) Now, imagine each time you go to hug them, they rush past you. They're too busy, too anxious, too distracted to stop and receive your love. How would that make you feel?

I paused. Then, I felt it: Rejected.

I was so busy pushing through that I never stopped to simply receive God's love and comfort, and this was grieving God.

JUST RECEIVE? What a concept.

The world is *so* demanding. Schedules, relationships, finances, what to eat, what not to eat. Fit that workout in. Go to church. Serve at church. Calm down! Hurry up! Show up! My gosh...no wonder every other ad I see is about high cortisol!

Holy Spirit whispered *just receive*...so, in that moment, I let it all go. I imagined all of my own perceived strength rolling out of my toes. Then, in quiet desperation, I asked the Holy Spirit to fill me with *His* strength. In the sacred stillness, I found something I hadn't known...real rest.

In pausing to be held by Him, a powerful exchange took place. I laid down my panic, and He wrapped me in His blessed peace.

After some time in this refreshing encounter, God told me to share what happened with Matt and the girls on our drive to California. So, I did, encouraging us all to spend the drive filling up with the love and peace of God to prepare our hearts for the unpredictable dynamics we were headed to.

Was the entire family weekend perfectly peaceful? No. But I was in a much better place. The Lord didn't change my circumstances; He changed me instead. I never showed up the same again. I also started saying no to things that had this effect on my soul, and I never had another panic attack.

Psalm 121:1 (NIV):
I lift up my eyes to the mountains—where does my help come from?

PowerSoul, allow the Holy Spirit to relieve you of whatever is causing you anxiety. Ask Him to forgive you for trying to handle it on your own. Then, be held. God is not disappointed when you come to Him weak. You are His beloved. He *wants* you to run to Him anytime you need to! You were not made to do any of this alone.

Giving all of your worries to God is connected to humility, releasing control and trusting Him.

1 Peter 5:6–7 (NLT):
So, humble yourselves under the mighty power of God, and at the right time he will lift you up in honor. Give all your worries and cares to God, for he cares about you.

Now, when I am stressed, I take time to receive.

Here is another visual I practice when I start to feel overwhelmed: I picture myself carrying my burdens in a heavy, large chest into a huge cathedral (representing heaven). Up the isle I walk to the Lord's feet. As I lay the chest down at His throne, I see His face light up with immense love for me. His eyes...so happy that I trust Him to take care the things I can't control and the problems that want to plague me. Then, I'm able to walk back out into the world, light, like a child, who isn't worried anymore because I KNOW My Father is working on my behalf.

2 Corinthians 12:9–10 (NLT):
"My grace is all you need. My power works best in weakness." So now I am glad to boast about my weaknesses, so that the power of Christ can work through me. That's why I take pleasure in my weaknesses, and in the insults, hardships, persecutions, and troubles that I suffer for Christ. For when I am weak, then I am strong.

POWER ⚡ SOUL PLUG-IN

Reveal

What is God speaking to me through this chapter?

Reflect

Where have I been trying to hold it all together instead of letting God hold me?

Respond

What burden, worry, or pressure do I need to place into God's hands today?

Power Move

Take ten quiet minutes to just receive.
Picture yourself laying every burden at God's feet, then sit still and let His peace meet you there.

Pray

Lord, I release what has been weighing me down.
Teach me to rest in Your love and receive Your strength in my weakness.
In Jesus' name, amen.

Declaration

I do not have to be strong on my own.
When I come to God weak, His power meets me there.

11

POWER OF THE SWORD

PROVERBS 18:21 (NLT):

The tongue can bring death or life; those who love to talk will reap the consequences.

When my girls were little, I would raise my voice a lot more than I should have. I wasn't always raging out of control, but yelling had become my default to get their attention. It made me feel heard, and at the time, I didn't think it was that big of a deal.

Until one day, right in the middle of correcting them, I saw my oldest daughter flinch when I raised my voice. It broke my heart.

I wasn't even that mad, but the scared look on her sweet face told a different story. In that moment, I saw it clearly. Even though my intentions weren't to hurt them, I was.

For years, they had watched me sit with my Bible and pen, watching Joyce Meyer spoon feed me the Word. I was committed to Christ and growing in my faith, but I was still losing the battle with my mouth. I wasn't exactly a shining example of transformation, reading my Bible in the morning and yelling like a crazy person by the afternoon.

Almost immediately, I could hear the enemy whispering, *You're such a bad mom. You're failing*. Of course, he would attack what mattered most to me.

I didn't want to hurt the people I loved. The Lord was so kind to show me that even when my frustration was understandable, the way I was expressing it was doing damage.

Our words, tone, and delivery matter. So I prayed, "Lord, break my heart every time I raise my voice without intention, until I stop."

And He answered.

I became painfully aware of how careless I could be with my mouth, not just with my girls, but everywhere. I couldn't control it on my own. I desperately needed the Holy Spirit's power to do what I could not.

JAMES 3:8 (NLT):
But no one can tame the tongue. It is restless and evil, full of deadly poison.

RESTLESS. EVIL. FULL OF DEADLY POISON. Are we hearing this warning? I was starting to.

LUKE 6:45 (NIV):
For the mouth speaks what the heart is full of.

That scripture says it all. Whatever we are full of will come out of our mouth.

One day, in the middle of another tirade, the Holy Spirit interrupted me with a simple but piercing question: *Whose voice are you echoing? Mine or the enemy's?*

I had been dwelling on the devil's whispers until they became my words. I had believed I needed to be intimidating to be heard and perfect to be a good mom. The enemy was pushing me to yell and then shaming me for doing it.

The truth was, I wasn't just a frustrated mom expressing emotion. I was releasing something spiritual. What I thought was disciplining my girls was actually my fears and insecurities spilling onto them.

Over time, God didn't just correct my words, He transformed what came out of my mouth. After years (really decades) of learning and applying the power of the tongue, God gave me a vision I will never forget.

As I prayed for my family one morning, I saw a gleaming sword coming out of my mouth. I was stunned. Then, the Holy Spirit spoke to my heart: *This is what the enemy sees now when you speak and pray in My authority.*

God had changed me. The same mouth I had once used to amplify the enemy's agenda was now being used to speak life, declare truth, and push back darkness.

Left on its own, the tongue can be destructive. But when it's surrendered to God and filled with His Word, it becomes powerful and life giving.

EPHESIANS 6:17 (NIV):
Take...the sword of the Spirit, which is the word of God.

Your tongue is a sword. God's Word is the only offensive weapon He has given us against the enemy and his schemes. But a sword only works when you pick it up and use it.

2 CORINTHIANS 10:3–5:
For though we walk in the flesh, we are not waging war according to the flesh. For the weapons of our warfare are not of the flesh but have divine power to destroy strongholds. We destroy arguments and every lofty opinion raised against the knowledge of God and take every thought captive to obey Christ.

So, we can't ignore or justify our thoughts. We can't let them run unchecked until they become our words. We don't just speak. We use God's truth to destroy lies and take authority over what tries to take root in our mind.

God can read our thoughts, but the enemy only hears what we say. So, we stay aware, we stay aligned, and we don't give the enemy an in.

Of course, I still fail. I talk a lot...

There are moments where our words wound. We react emotionally instead of responding with wisdom. What comes out of our mouths doesn't always reflect the heart of God, or even our own. The good news is, He will correct us in a powerful yet loving way.

He wants us to win. He wants us to cut off the liar and speak words of truth with love that heal and encourage. He never gives up on us, so we don't give up either. Jesus took your guilt and shame to the cross, so don't carry your past.

Pick up your sword. Speak life. Let your words reflect who you are now.

POWER ⚡ SOUL PLUG-IN

Reveal
What is God speaking to me through this chapter?

Reflect
What have my words been producing lately: healing, peace, and truth, or fear, damage, and discouragement?

Respond
What is one pattern in my speech that God is asking me to surrender and replace with His truth?

Power Move
Before you speak in a tense moment this week, pause and ask, Will these words help or harm?

Pray
Lord, please forgive me for speaking anything that breaks Your heart or does not align with You. Purify my heart and govern my mouth. Let my thoughts be rooted in Your truth, and may my words overflow with life.
In Jesus' name, amen.

Declaration
I take every thought captive and bring it into obedience to Christ.
I cancel every negative or evil agreement I've spoken over myself or others.
My tongue is no longer a weapon for the enemy. I speak blessings, not curses.
My words will honor the Lord.

12

POWER OF ONE

Proverbs 16:9:

In their hearts humans plan their course, but the Lord establishes their steps.

Before I opened my eyes, half-dreaming and half-awake, I saw a vision of a giant roller coaster.

I could almost feel the click, click, click up the steep climb to the sudden rush and stomach drop. Before I could make sense of it, I heard in my spirit, *Things are about to get crazy. Hold on to Me.*

My heart swelled with anticipation. *Here it is. MY moment. MY launch. MY breakthrough* (me, me, me)! I had no idea how literal God's warning was. The entire world was about to twist and turn like never before.

A short time after that vision, God had asked me to do something that made absolutely no sense: to plan an event. And not a small gathering...a full-scale, ticketed event with speakers at a resort venue.

The problem was, I had no ministry following or email list. I did not have a large online audience. Just a few hundred social media friends. But I couldn't shake the instruction. I knew it was God.

So, I rolled up my sleeves and jumped headfirst into planning the PowerSoul Experience. I booked the resort, confirmed the speakers, and started promoting. Everything looked set for a launch that would *have* to be miraculous because in the natural; there was no way I could fill that ballroom.

Enter the rollercoaster: COVID-19.

At first, I thought it would pass quickly. "Two weeks to slow the spread," they said. So, I kept planning and stayed hopeful. I even joked online that we'd cover our masks in glitter...Michael Jackson style.

It was hard enough to pack a venue WITHOUT a pandemic, but I was committed to seeing this through, even though the pressure was mounting.

Then, the resort called. They were legally barred from hosting events. My contract was canceled. The event that the Lord insisted I plan, dissolved.

Deep down, I was relieved. I started to realize that God knew the whole time that the world would shut down. He knew the ballroom would never have to be filled. He knew this assignment was never about the event. It was always about my obedience. The offering wasn't the outcome. It was all about my *yes* to obey when things looked completely impossible.

So, instead of a resort conference, I hosted an online PowerSoul Experience to encourage those stuck at home. I'm not sure how many people watched it, but I'm sure God saw my willingness to follow Him into the unknown.

After that, I planned our first in-person gathering outside at a local park. It was a beautiful sunny Arizona day. My best friend Kellie and I packed blankets, filled our hydro flasks, and prepared a message. I pictured women spread across the large grass area, receiving power for their souls!

We prepared space for a crowd. Three women showed up.

Three of my beautiful high-school friends arrived, probably just out of curiosity. For a moment, I was disappointed. I felt like the Lord prompted me to plan these things, so I was a confused when more women didn't show up. I had imagined momentum. Instead, it was the five of us, sitting in a small circle in a large empty field.

But then, God came. The Holy Spirit wrapped around us like a warm, weighted blanket...thick, comforting, unmistakably present. It felt like those big parachutes we used to play with in school, when we'd throw them into the air and then run underneath as they floated down over us. Heaven covered our little circle.

Afterward, we climbed into my truck, and Kellie turned to me wide-eyed and exclaimed, "DID YOU FEEL THAT?!"

I nodded. "Yes! The presence of God was here!"

As we drove away, the Holy Spirit spoke to my heart again: *I want to know you'll do this even if only one person shows up.*

It was a question that stripped away performance and comparison. Would I still plan a gathering, prepare the message, create space, and obey for only one person? Or maybe what He was asking if I would move just for Him.

That day, I decided ***I will live for an audience of One.*** No more measuring success by the world's standards.

Maybe you're building something right now that looks small, unimpressive, or feels like a failure. Don't assume you missed

God. If He has called you to it, don't quit. Sometimes the launch isn't about the crowd, it's about your character. Your obedience isn't measured by earthly applause. It's measured by faith. Sometimes the empty room is where God builds the greatest leaders.

God is our audience. Don't get caught up in self-promotion. Ask the Lord to energize you for your next steps. Do your part and leave the rest to Him. And when it's time, He'll promote you. He happens to be the greatest promoter of all time. He kinda knows everyone!

Zechariah 4:10:
Do not despise these small beginnings, for the Lord rejoices to see the work begin.

POWER SOUL PLUG-IN

Reveal
What is God speaking to me through this chapter?

Reflect
Where have I been measuring success by numbers, applause, visibility, or results instead of simple obedience to God?

Respond
What would I do differently if God alone was my audience?

Power Move
Do one act of obedience this week that no one may notice or celebrate.
Do it wholeheartedly as an offering to God.

Pray
Lord, free me from comparison, performance, and the need for recognition.
Teach me to live faithfully before You alone.
In Jesus' name, amen.

Declaration
My obedience is not validated by crowds or applause.
God is my audience, and faithfulness is success.

13

POWER YOUR SOUL

Matthew 18:20:

For where two or three gather together in my name, there am I with them.

While the world was masking up and standing six feet apart, the Spirit stirred up something new in me.

My heart grew heavy as I listened to my clients, over Zoom calls, describe the negative ripple effects of the pandemic on them and their households. Some were homeschooling for the first time. Some were desperately trying to keep their jobs. Most weren't used to being home with their spouse and kids around the clock. And hanging over all of it was a palpable global tension with an undercurrent of fear and stress that seemed to seep into everything.

Pacing my living room and praying, I asked the Lord what I should do. I didn't want to sit in my house, helpless. I needed to do something. *Lord, do I volunteer at church?* (My church had reopened.)

No...that wasn't it.

But one thing was clear: women needed each other now more than ever, and so instead of overthinking it, I created what I would want if I was depressed and climbing the walls of my house. I would want my girlfriends, tacos, a margarita, and Jesus.

When PowerSoul first launched, it wasn't a carefully orchestrated vision with a five-year plan and an event team. With God stirring my spirit, it was my very hospitable husband Matt and me making space for women to encounter Him in a new way.

The first PowerSoul Clubhouse gathering (after the park) happened in our home—a condo that feels like a little glass treehouse in the sky. Bright. Urban. And wide open to the most incredible Arizona sunsets. When I looked around at what I had, I didn't see lack. I saw a special place. An altar.

We used what we had to make space for what God wanted to do. And just like that, 15 women showed up. Hungry for tacos, sure, but they were even more hungry for something new and fun. They knew this would be different from the polished, performative church circles they'd tiptoed through for years.

I've been there. Sitting at a round-table study with a styrofoam cup of coffee, where wearing a concert T-shirt might get you labeled a "baby Christian" and earn a few judgmental glances. And like many women, there were years when getting to Sunday morning church was a handful. I'd rush to get us all ready, wrangle my daughters into kids club, and finally slip into service to sit behind a woman rubbing her husband's back the entire time. Probably in hopes that he would want to come back the next week. Ugh...

I wanted PowerSoul Clubhouse to be a place where women didn't have to stress or bring anything but themselves. A place they could come as they are, relax, have fun and be loved by Christ.

I'm not *at all* saying we shouldn't be a part of our local church or that all round-table Bible studies are judgmental and boring. I'm just saying that spending time with other believers doesn't always have to look the same way. The Word says that when two or more are gathered, "...I am with them."

People of God, we ARE the church.

God showed me early on that I was called to the "gap" space between the organized church and the world, and now I get it.

I'm here for women who pour out all week and aren't looking for one more responsibility. I'm here for the woman who finds most small talk exhausting. I'm here for the woman who may dress a bit more edgy or creative than the church crowd. I'm here for the woman who might never pursue a pew but would run to happy hour with her friends in a heartbeat.

So, I gave God what was in my hands, and He has given us encounters where His presence could not be denied.

One night, after sharing God's Word, I was giving my testimony about when I hit rock bottom in the panic attack. I turned down the lights to walk them through the activation that had been so helpful to me:

"Close your eyes," I said. "Picture that one thing...your biggest fear, your private burden, the thing you're begging God to help you with. Now, imagine all of your own strength, your stress and your striving draining from your body. Let it flow out of your mind, shoulders, chest, and stomach till it all runs out of the tips of your toes. Let it go. Now, invite the Holy Spirit and ask Him to fill you with His strength and His power.

Let His peace overwhelm you...breathe...rest in Him."

And then came the music.

I had a soft worship song queued up. But as I stood there, the Holy Spirit kept prompting something else: *Play the Adele song*.

I resisted. I had played it before and didn't want to be repetitive. But the Spirit pressed. So, I played it: "Make You Feel My Love."

I asked the women to receive each word not from Adele, but from God. The words washed over everyone as if He was singing them directly to our hearts. The room went silent except for some sniffles.

After I was done speaking, a woman came up to me in tears. "I've never experienced anything like this," she said. "When that song played, I lost it. That was mine and my husband's song when we first met."

She went on to tell me that her marriage was really struggling, but in that moment, God reminded her of when their love was new. The Lord was saying, "I see you." He was restoring her hope as she felt the presence and power of God's love. I heard later that her marriage began to heal.

This is my *why*.

So, yes, we serve margaritas. And yes, sometimes we play secular music. But when women come to this "ultimate happy hour," they also see me open my Bible in a way that feels relatable and they hear the truth about Jesus. Like Him challenging the Pharisees of His time, I would rather be Spirit-led and misunderstood than religiously safe.

God isn't looking for polished religion. He's looking for true surrender. He's looking for what's real. And in my experience, that's what most people are looking for too.

So, I am willing to do the unconventional if that's what it takes to meet women right where they are. And just for the record, no one is getting drunk at our clubhouse on anything but the power of the Holy Spirit.

Because when God wants to reach His daughters, He will do it in a bar, a beauty salon, or a borrowed living room. He will do it through a secular song that suddenly turns sacred. He will even use a rascal like me...because He wants to use the rascals too.

Luke 5:32 (NLT):
I have come to call not those who think they are righteous, but those who know they are sinners and need to repent.

POWER ⚡ SOUL PLUG-IN

Reveal
What is God speaking to me through this chapter?

Reflect
Have I been waiting for perfect timing or perfect conditions before letting God use me?

Respond
What can I offer God right now, exactly as things are?

Power Move
Use what is already available to you this week.
Open your table, send the invitation, encourage a friend, host the gathering, or create space for connection and God's presence.

Pray
Lord, show me what You have already provided and teach me to use it for Your purposes.
Help me make room for people to encounter Your love.
In Jesus' name, amen.

Declaration
I do not need perfect conditions to be used by God.
What I place in His hands becomes a place of healing, connection, and transformation.

14

POWER OF ALIGNMENT

GALATIANS 1:10 (NLT):

Obviously, I'm not trying to win the approval of people, but of God. If pleasing people were my goal, I would not be Christ's servant.

PowerSoul Clubhouse started to grow. One night after we gathered, my dear friend Kristie Sexton pulled me aside and said, "I have a surprise for you." With a smile, she told me she had a contact at Faith Talk Radio and had told them about me and what I was building with PowerSoul. "Would you want your own radio show?"

My jaw dropped. "Ummmmm...YA!"

A few weeks later, I found myself inside Arizona's Salem Studios about to launch *The PowerSoul Show*. I sat down for a sound check, headset on, mic in front of me. The moment I heard my voice through those headphones, something clicked.

As a little girl, I used to swing on the swing set in my backyard for hours, singing and dreaming. I would imagine myself on a stage or on TV, using my voice. In the '70s and '80s, if you wanted to be heard, you had to be a singer, actress, or model...or so I thought. I tried some of that, and I was not terrible at it, but none of it felt right.

I remember being 11 years old when I finally heard a recording of my own singing voice, and it was not good. Definitely not variety show material. But still, I had a knowing that never left me. I was meant to be in front of a crowd.

And here I was all these years later, hearing my voice through the headphones. Not singing or performing, just speaking. And God whispered, *This is like hearing your instrument for the very first time.*

I felt the anointing and God's green light. I was finally aligned with my calling. God had told me years before to get ready to speak, and now I actually had a place to speak from.

I started sharing stories about faith, freedom, and breakthrough. Encouragement flowed through the airwaves in the aftermath of covid and the fear that gripped the nation. I couldn't avoid the hard topics that some people would rather leave alone. Staying safe may have been easier, but that is not what God called me to.

And looking back, I can see how every step of alignment positioned me for doors and relationships I never could have planned. Not because I was trying to be controversial, but because I was committed to staying aligned. I wasn't going to water it down or make it more palatable. Even the early Clubhouse promotions made it clear:

CLUBHOUSE RULES:

WE LOVE JESUS
WE LOVE OUR COUNTRY
WE ENCOURAGE EACH OTHER
WE CHOOSE FAITH OVER FEAR
WE HAVE FUN
WE POWERSOUL!

I figured having rules meant no one was blindsided if they showed up.

As PowerSoul grew, so did my network and my coaching business. God kept opening doors. One of those doors was through a client who introduced me to a fabulous socialite who embodied both words to the max. Social and lit. Her name is Tina Hillstrom.

Tina invited me and Matt to attend a black-tie event at Mar-a-Lago, President Donald Trump's private residence. It was surreal. We met superstars from the conservative movement like Judge Jeanine Pirro, Jon Voight, and Mike Lindell.

Already in awe, country legend Lee Greenwood took the stage and started to sing "Proud to Be an American." Tears filled my eyes as I was overwhelmed with gratitude. Gratitude for my country, for freedom, and for the divine opportunities God was orchestrating. I couldn't stop thinking, *How did we get here?*

Traveling home, I had chills for hours. I thought I might be getting sick but felt fine. I realized it was not illness. It was the Holy Spirit, present and tangible in the best way.

During the days of lockdown and beyond, I became social media friends with Kari Lake. Yes, the news anchor from Arizona who has become a national voice for mama bears around the country. We sent each other memes that made us laugh during a not-so-funny time. So aligned in our thinking, our DMs turned into a real friendship.

I found out she was being awarded Woman of the Year here in Arizona and decided to attend. When we met eyes across the room, she ran toward me yelling, "Brandie!" We hugged like old friends. Instant sisters.

Our stories parallel in so many ways. Both of us were called out of our comfortable careers to step into territory we did not ask for but knew God was calling us into. Both of us had counted the cost of saying yes and followed God onto a battlefield.

Soon, I was co-hosting a political radio show on Patriot 960 AM, interviewing modern-day freedom fighters. None of them had intended to become political either. They were simply willing to speak truth even when it cost them something.

On July 4, 2021, Kari hosted her very first rally after announcing her run for Arizona governor. July in Arizona is scorching hot, so most Phoenicians escape to the mountains or the beach. Surprisingly, a huge crowd of patriots packed the ballroom, ready for a political shift. Kari was not just launching her campaign. She was taking a stand for her God-given assignment.

I was proud of her and thrilled when she asked me to open the rally. Backstage, Kari asked if we could huddle and pray. And then it was time. The room was overflowing.

Just like a PowerSoul night, I began with a song to break the ice and bring joy.

A couple of verses in, the music cut out. Dead silent.

Let me be clear. When I play songs, I sing over them to bring up the energy, but I am not actually singing them. So, there I was, hundreds in the ballroom, thousands watching online, news cameras flashing, microphone in my hand, lyrics playing on the screen behind me, but no sound.

In a second, I had a choice to make. Do I shrink back, or do I lean in and sing? I sang. Not because I have the best voice, but because it was not about me. It was about the message. I knew discouraged people needed to hear those words. I had to push past the fear of embarrassment for a greater purpose.

Later, Kari told me, "I was backstage in shock. I thought, who is this woman?!" She still laughs about it. It made an impression. People still come up to me and talk about it.

Ultimately, my reputation cannot be more important than the message. If I am going to walk in alignment with God's call on my life, I have to lay down what people may think. And let me tell you...people had thoughts.

Later that night, I watched the livestream comments:

Who is this chick, and why is she speaking?

She looks plastic.

Too much Botox.

The comments went on and on, and it stung. But the worst was not from strangers. The worst came from people I loved and thought were in my corner. That's what really hurt. I expected attacks from the enemy. I did not expect them from people I once called friends.

It felt like I took a roundhouse kick to the face. One minute I was standing strong, in my element, having a blast. The next, I was curled up on the couch, wounded and in pain. But even then, I knew I was in alignment. I knew I was doing what God called me to do. That is the cost sometimes. Rejection. Misunderstanding.

Obedience can be expensive. But when you fully align with God's will for your life, somcthing shifts. You become anchored. He fills you with purpose. And He gives you a peace that does not depend on people's approval.

Yes, there is a cost to alignment. But there is also anointing. And anointing is not something you want to live without.

God's anointing is the presence and power of the Holy Spirit on a person for a specific purpose. Your talent does not anoint you. Your influence does not anoint you. Only God anoints.

The enemy will try to pressure you into perfection so you never move. Or fear will convince you to stay quiet. Either way, if you care more about what people think than what God said, you have put them in a place they were never meant to be.

Take them off His throne. They do not belong there.

Romans 8:31 (NLT):
What shall we say about such wonderful things as these? If God is for us, who can ever be against us?

POWER ⚡ SOUL PLUG-IN

Reveal
What is God speaking to me through this chapter?

Reflect
Where have I been valuing people's approval, comfort, or fear of criticism more than obedience to God?

Respond
What is one area of my life where I know God is asking for deeper alignment right now?

Power Move
Take a moment and imagine lying on your deathbed with no time left.
Are you satisfied with how you lived?
Did you live the life you were made for?

Pray
Lord, free me from fear, distraction, and the need for approval.
Give me courage to live fully aligned with Your will and without regret.
In Jesus' name, amen.

Declaration
I will not be ruled by fear, people-pleasing, or rejection.
I am anchored in God's call, and His anointing is worth the cost.

14

POWER OF COVERING

Psalm 91:1–2 (NLT):

Those who live in the shelter of the Most High will find rest in the shadow of the Almighty. This I declare about the Lord: He alone is my refuge, my place of safety; He is my God, and I trust Him.

I think you can see how I have a heart for the wild ones and would even call myself a rebel with a cause. But dressing funky or having an occasional margarita is different than rebellion against God. Blatant rebellion is unwise. In fact, it's dangerous.

Picture a beautiful ranch. Wide-open land. Mountains in the distance. Sunlight stretching across golden fields and rows of stables filled with well cared for horses.

Inside the rancher's fence, everything is provided: shelter, food, protection, and loving care. The rancher knows every horse by name. He feeds them, brushes them, tends to their wounds, and watches over them.

God is the Rancher. We are His horses.

But outside the fence, another group roams: the wild, rebellious horses. They watch from a distance. They see the provision and the peaceful life the rancher gives, but they refuse one thing: the Rancher's bit of submission. To the wild horse, the bit looks like control and losing freedom. It looks like weakness. But to have the beautiful life the Rancher offers, a horse must come under His full authority and submit.

The word submission just sounds oppressive, doesn't it? Like being pinned down, pressured, or forced to give in, like those childhood arm-wrestling matches where you cry, "Mercy!" before someone almost breaks your wrist.

I believe much of the world sees coming into a submissive relationship with an Almighty God that way. But in God's Kingdom, submission is something completely different. Before I understood this, I lived in a season where I convinced myself I could do my own thing without consequence. I loved the Lord very much, but I was also knowingly resisting His ways.

In this season, I was divorced and dating Matt. I had a small apartment where Matt stayed over almost every night. We were sleeping together, and I knew it was wrong, but I justified it because we loved each other. I saw my future with him, so I told myself God knew my heart. Yet I knew I was openly disobeying what God says in His Word. And just because I loved Matt did not mean God stopped being holy and having holy standards. The world calls living and sleeping together normal. God calls it sin.

Proverbs 14:12 (NLT):
There is a way that seems right to a person, but its end is the way to death.

Notice it does not say the path looks wrong. It says it seems right. That is what makes it so dangerous. The road can feel reasonable and loving. It can even feel responsible. From the outside, nothing about it looks reckless.

That is how compromise usually begins. One of my favorite pastors, Tom Schrader, used to say, "The road to hell is a gradual one." We rarely wake up one morning and decide to rebel against God. It usually starts with a small step that feels harmless. We explain it away. We tell ourselves our situation is different. We convince ourselves God understands.

Little by little, what once bothered our conscience becomes normal, and before long, the line we once promised we would never cross is somewhere behind us. Most of the time, the real struggle is not that we do not know what God has said. The struggle is that we do know, and we are trying to make peace with ignoring it.

That is why this verse is so sobering. What seems right in the moment is not always the path that leads to the victorious life we want.

Here I was, asking God for His blessings while living outside the very boundaries that carried His protection. At the same time, I was a single mom. Jadelyn was just a toddler. Each morning, I dropped her at preschool, went straight to aesthetics school, and then my mom picked her up in the afternoons so I could wait tables late into the night. I was exhausted and emotionally drained and just wanted to be "happy." I wasn't trying to rebel; I was trying to survive. And comfort has a way of becoming a counterfeit savior when you're tired enough.

Then came New Year's Eve, 1999—the night we stepped into a new millennium. We were invited to an over-the-top party with a famous DJ, multiple bars, even a full seafood spread under a huge tent. Pretty extravagant for a group of 20 somethings.

Before we left my apartment that night, I had prayed for God to protect us. Not long after we arrived, I took a small amount of ecstasy, another compromise, but instead of amplifying the fun, the mercy of God used it to reveal the spiritual darkness all around me. I could see the evil. People all drugged up, dancing and disappearing into back rooms, an atmosphere I had never experienced before. I had to leave.

I grabbed Matt's hand and pulled him outside. He could tell something was wrong. I tried to explain what I was seeing and sensing all around. Then I said, "This isn't me. Living like this, being here, doing things this way...this isn't who I am." I loved Matt deeply, but I wanted God's hand on our lives much more than I wanted adrenaline, comfort, or control.

Before we met, Matt loved his bachelor life as a hockey player who had moved from state to state, avoiding serious relationships. And I had just come out of a commitment that had gone painfully wrong. We were both afraid of marriage. Still, I told him that if we were going to continue, there was only one way forward, and it meant honoring God. It meant surrender. It meant submission. Matt agreed.

So, we set a date on the calendar for the following year.

A few months later, I found out I was pregnant with our daughter Chloe'. Now I was a pregnant single mom, finishing school, working nights, raising a toddler, and living with constant uncertainty...and morning sickness.

I remember sitting outside of my aesthetics school one afternoon on a break with my head in my hands, thinking about how messed up my life was. I was at the end of myself, and I looked up toward God and recommitted my life to Him. I was done doing things my way.

We were married a month later on a small yacht in the San Diego harbor with 40 of our closest friends and family. Our entire wedding cost less than $5,000. It wasn't elaborate, but it was truly special. We understood that it wasn't about a flamboyant wedding and reception. It was about our vows to God and each other.

At sunset, on the bow of the boat, we asked for the Rancher's blessing and leadership over our lives and came under His glorious covering.

Submission didn't diminish my life; it stabilized. Looking back, I'm convinced that our decision to marry when we did opened the door for God to bless our life together over and over again.

If you've spent your life running wild and on the edge, "the stable" might sound boring. Where's the passion, the drama, the action? It may make for soap operas, but if you've ever been around someone who lives that way, it gets exhausting fast.

The devil wants to entice you with adrenaline and what seems exciting to your flesh. God wants you high on His Spirit, living in peace. Take it from me, the chaos and confusion of living outside of God's covering is not a good time. Once you've experienced the steady hand of the Rancher guiding your life, you realize something the rebellious will never understand.

The greatest adventure of your life begins inside the fence.

Deuteronomy 28:1–2 (NLT):
If you fully obey the Lord your God and carefully keep all His commands... the Lord your God will set you high above all the nations of the world. You will experience all these blessings if you obey the Lord your God.

POWER SOUL PLUG-IN

Reveal
What is God speaking to me through this chapter?

Reflect
Where in my life have I mistaken compromise for freedom?

Respond
What is one area of my life where God is inviting me back under His protection and authority?

Power Move
Identify any compromise God has been highlighting.
Make concrete change this week that brings your life back into alignment with His truth.

Pray
Lord, please forgive me for my rebellion against you. I do not want to live outside of Your best for me. Lead me, correct me, and teach me to trust Your ways above my own.
In Jesus' name, amen.

Declaration
God loves me and His boundaries are good. I am blessed as I submit myself to Him.

15

POWER OF YOUR CIRCLE

Proverbs 13:20:

Walk with the wise and become wise;
associate with fools and get in trouble.

When I started to really pursue God's purpose for my life, some of my close relationships started to feel strained. There was either a falling out or just a strange tension I couldn't ignore. I wanted to brush it off and tell myself it was just a season. But it was more than that.

With each interaction, I began to feel like I could no longer be myself. I had outgrown the same conversations that circled around and around. For years, I had participated in dwelling on the past and criticizing the same people. Gossip felt like camaraderie until one day it didn't.

I remember sitting there listening to the same conversation again, and suddenly I wasn't laughing anymore. My spirit felt heavy. It started to feel gross and dark, like my soul was craving sunshine but my circle only met in the basement. I stopped thinking it was fun. I could see how stuck we all were and how it broke God's heart. I was convicted, and I knew I wanted more.

I've said this before, but I'll say it again. Believing in Jesus is one thing. Following Him means your life will start to look different. **Following Him means leveling up.**

Think of a glorious penthouse with massive skylights and fresh air. The more time I spent with the Lord, the more the basement bothered me. This didn't mean I stopped loving people who I was close to. It was because of my deep love for them that my soul grieved. When I stopped coming around as often, it looked like I was rejecting them. And the enemy was quick to try and guilt me. Sometimes that guilt even came through messengers who said things like, "You aren't being a good Christian."

But it was the Lord who told us to guard our hearts, and He helped me understand something important: I wasn't rejecting people. I was following Him. That meant leaving sinful habits and a destructive mindset. He also revealed something else: everyone choosing the basement has access to the same elevator.

Scripture warns us about the influence people have on our lives. First Corinthians says this:

1 Corinthians 15:33:
Do not be deceived: Bad company corrupts good character.

You've probably heard the saying that you become the average of the five people you spend the most time with. It sounds like one of those catchy clichés people repeat, but there's scientific truth behind it. Researchers have discovered that habits, attitudes, and even emotional states spread through close relationships.

If the people around you smoke, you're far more likely to smoke. If the people around you are constantly negative and complain, you will too. If a close friend gains weight, your chances of gaining weight increase dramatically. I guess misery loves company...AND snacks.

The people closest to you will eventually influence which floor you end up living on. Joy spreads. Depression spreads. So do destructive patterns. Freedom and bondage are both contagious.

I've watched sincere, faith-filled Christians miss out on the abundant life Jesus died to give them because they never learned to see themselves the way He does. Instead of seeing themselves as redeemed and called up higher, they begin to identify more with their wounds and dysfunction. When healing feels too hard and change seems too costly, people naturally drift toward environments where no one challenges them. It feels easier. Feelings rule them, so they surround themselves with people who prefer the version of them that stays numb, small, and stuck. Birds of a feather really do stick together, and they rarely celebrate the one who leaves the hen house and decides to fly higher.

But when you surround yourself with people who pursue freedom and desire to look more like Christ, their character calls you higher.

One of my favorite moments in Scripture shows exactly what the right kind of friendship looks like. In Mark chapter 2, Jesus was teaching inside a crowded house in Capernaum. People filled every inch of the room and spilled out the doorway just to hear Him. Four men arrived carrying a paralyzed friend on a mat. They believed that if they could just get him to Jesus, everything could change.

The house was so full they couldn't get through the door. Most people would have turned around, but not these friends. They climbed onto the roof, made an opening, and lowered their friend down into the middle of the room right in front of Jesus. The Bible says that when Jesus saw their faith, He told the man to get up, pick up his mat, and walk.

And he did! He was no longer paralyzed because his faithful friends were determined to carry him closer to Jesus!

Real friendship doesn't hold someone down when they're trying to get up. It doesn't resent growth or mock the person who wants more for their life. Real friends want to see you whole, healthy, and free. They don't compete with your healing or feel threatened when you begin to change. They help you toward it!

Now, think about the people closest to you. Are they the kind of friends who help carry you closer to Jesus or the kind who leave you lying on the mat because they're lying there too?

I know the power of the right circle because I've experienced it myself. Being around the right people has strengthened me when I've been weak. My close friends refuse to let me settle in a pit. They contend for my breakthroughs, and I contend for theirs.

From the beginning, God said it was not good for man to be alone. Throughout Scripture, His people are never described as isolated individuals but as one body with many parts moving together. **When healthy believers gather in community, faith spreads.**

This is also why the enemy works so hard to isolate people. Alone, you are more vulnerable. But in the right circle, you are stronger.

I've watched this happen in our PowerSoul plug-ins (our small group meetings). Women walk in burdened and leave lighter because the group spoke life, prayed boldly, and reminded them who they are.

Up in the penthouse, people still have and express real struggles, but the conversations are different. They focus on growth and what God is doing instead of rehearsing defeat. They encourage one another and celebrate breakthrough. That's the power of your circle.

You really can't stay neutral. So, choose light. Choose freedom. Choose a circle with values that move you closer to Jesus.

Joshua 24:15 (NLT):
Choose today whom you will serve… But as for me and my family, we will serve the LORD.

POWER ⚡ SOUL PLUG-IN

Reveal
What is God speaking to me through this chapter?

Reflect
Who are the five people I spend the most time with right now? Do they reflect who I want to become in Christ?

Respond
Where might God be asking me to make a change so I can grow and live in freedom?

Power Move
Identify one relationship, habit, or environment that consistently pulls you lower.
Then take one step this week toward the kind of circle that calls you higher.

Pray
Lord, open my eyes to see the influence of my circle.
Give me wisdom to surround myself with friendships that honor You and the call on my life.
Give me courage to walk away from anything hindering my walk with You.
In Jesus' name, amen.

Declaration
I will not settle for circles that keep me stuck.
God is leading me into relationships that strengthen my faith and call me higher.

16

POWER OF BOUNDARIES

Proverbs 4:23:

Above all else, guard your heart, for everything you do flows from it.

When I was younger, I had no idea what a boundary was. I grew up in a family that was extremely close. Everyone knew everyone's business ALL of the time. That was my normal. I thought being immersed in each other's drama meant love.

As I got older and my own family began to mature, I started to feel the weight of not knowing where I ended and others began. On weekends we would run around from one obligation to another, not leaving much time for ourselves. I was drowning in people-pleasing because I didn't want to disappoint anyone and would end up taking it out on my husband.

When my marriage reached a breaking point, I realized something had to change. I couldn't keep saying yes to everyone else while saying no to the family God had called me to. And in that season, God gave me a vision:

In my mind's eye, I saw a beautiful garden. At the center was a cute little house on a strong foundation. The foundation was Jesus. Inside the house was my most sacred space (my heart): my husband, my children, and me, dwelling together with the fire of the Holy Spirit crackling in the fireplace...

Then, I saw a beautiful garden surrounding my house. The garden represented where I should sow seeds of time, money, and energy. Where I cultivate close relationships with people who truly loved me and didn't step on my roses when my back was turned. Those who valued me and my family and loved what God was building.

Around the garden, I saw a boundary...a white picket fence with a gate. This beautiful area was reserved for the ones who protect my peace. Only those who had proven trustworthy were invited inside.

Beyond the picket fence was an open prairie that represented a space for acquaintances, casual friendships, coworkers. You know, the ones you invite to share in the occasional barbecue but weren't assigned to my inner circle.

Then, beyond that was the barbed wire fence. Hanging on it was a "No Trespassing" sign. This represented the boundary line for people who meant me and my family harm. People whose words, actions, or alignment with the enemy would bring destruction if allowed too close. Letting them on my property would not be wise, even if I loved them.

That vision was ground-breaking for me.

BOUNDARIES ARE ABOUT ACCESS

The Lord showed me that most of us have never been taught to rightly divide who belongs where on our territory. Many times, we open gates God never told us to open. We give access to people who were never meant to have that kind of influence on us.

We let the wrong people wreak havoc on our lives because we are more concerned about disappointing them than obeying

God. So, we continue to waste our precious time and energy while they trample through, causing all kinds of suffering.

Some people really aren't thinking about how their actions affect you. Others are fully aware and do not care. And some are snakes who hope to see you stay stuck or suffer. Snakes don't have ears to hear God or correction, just venom in their mouths.

I don't know about you, but I don't want to tiptoe around my garden because snakes are waiting to strike. I don't want immature bugs picking at my harvest. And I don't want my flowers getting crushed under the feet of careless people with no respect for me and what I value.

And yet, that's exactly what happens when we don't guard what God has given us.

Galatians 1:10 (NLT):
Obviously, I'm not trying to win the approval of people, but of God. If pleasing people were my goal, I would not be Christ's servant.

BOUNDARIES ARE PROTECTION

Boundaries allow us to cultivate the right relationships, invest in the right places, and walk out our assignment with clarity and peace. Only when we have and maintain proper boundaries can our lives flourish the way God intended.

Those who truly love you will always want you to follow Him above following them. They will bless your life, not curse it. Not everyone is meant to have full access to your life, and that doesn't mean you stop loving them. It means you guard your heart and let God show you where they belong.

There are people God may call you to love, support, or even minister to closely. But assignment is not the same as access. Being called to help someone does not mean they belong in the spaces you are responsible to protect.

There are people who want to control you.

People who want to use you for their advantage.

People who will drain your energy because they don't know how to depend on God.

People who will try to keep you stuck because of their own fears.

People who carry jealousy and malice in their hearts toward you.

None of that is love. And sometimes the most powerful thing we can do is pray for people and get out of God's way.

THE PRUNING

One of the hardest things to do is move someone from the garden to the No Trespassing zone, especially when it's someone you once trusted and loved (and maybe you still do). To change their level of access can feel like loss, even when it is obedience.

Matthew 19:29 (NLT):
And everyone who has given up houses or brothers or sisters or father or mother or children or property, for my sake, will receive a hundred times as much in return and will inherit eternal life.

This may sound familiar, but it needs to be reinforced:

When people curse what God is blessing or dishonor what He's assigned, God will prune.

God sees the heart of everyone around you. When He removes relationships that no longer align with your calling, He is making space for His goodness to grow in and around you. Pruning doesn't mean God wants you to be harsh or unloving. It just means adjusting their access in your life, removing what is unhealthy, out of alignment, or hindering growth so something stronger and more fruitful can take its place.

I remember a story my daughter once told me about one of her teachers. He was an awesome man who would tell his students the story about the day his son, who was addicted to drugs, came to his door with a raw steak he had stolen and asked if he could grill it in his backyard.

His father said no, not because he didn't love him, but because he *did*.

He had a boundary: if his son would not choose to get clean, he could no longer have access to the home where his other siblings also lived and would be terribly affected.

His son died shortly after.

The teacher would tell this story in hopes of keeping his students safe from ever doing drugs. He told it even though it still caused him deep pain, believing his son's life and death could still impact the world for good.

I have stories of when holding a boundary and pruning has caused me to grieve too. But like the story above, pruning may be painful, but it is always purposeful.

PRUNING OR PRIDE? DISCERN THE DIFFERENCE

Discernment is key because not every separation is obedience.

It's entirely different when we distance ourselves from people out of pride rather than pruning. Sometimes we don't walk away because God is removing them; we walk away because they're calling us higher and we're not ready to change.

There are people who genuinely love you and want the best for you. Some have more life experience and can see pitfalls ahead before you do. Some know the Word of God more deeply. And sometimes they're not trying to control you at all but want to help and protect you.

To cut those people off because correction feels uncomfortable is not discernment. It's avoidance and rebellion against wisdom.

That is not the same as God Himself pruning relationships that no longer belong in your story or when He establishes boundaries to protect you. This is where the guidance of the Holy Spirit and the humility to walk with Him matter.

I am not an advocate for cutting people off simply because we disagree or go through a rough patch. But I do believe that when someone is consistently disrupting your peace, weakening your walk with God, or interfering with sacred moments in your life, it's time to re-evaluate and reset boundaries.

I opened this chapter with Proverbs 4:23 because it is such a STRONG scripture that tells us to guard our hearts above all else because everything in our life flows from what we allow to take root inside of us.

THE FRUIT TEST

How do you know what kind of access to give others? Jesus said you will know them by their fruit.

Galatians 5:22–23 (NLT):
But the Holy Spirit produces this kind of fruit in our lives: love, joy, peace, patience, kindness, goodness, faith-fulness, gentleness, and self-control. There is no law against these things!

It took me a long time to see that it doesn't matter much when someone says all the right things or calls themselves a Christian. **Even the devil can quote Scripture, so words are not enough.**

When I'm unsure, I bring it to God and look at the fruit.

Does this person consistently exhibit:

LOVE?
JOY?
PEACE?
PATIENCE?
KINDNESS?
GOODNESS?
FAITHFULNESS?
GENTLENESS?
SELF-CONTROL?

Matthew 7:16 (NLT):
You can identify them by their fruit, that is, by the way they act. Can you pick grapes from thornbushes, or figs from thistles?

God always produces GOOD fruit. And peace, not pride, is one of the clearest signs you're listening to Him.

ROOTED IN CHRIST

When we're children, we are planted in a family tree. But when we belong to Jesus, we are replanted into His family tree. Our primary identity is no longer found in family approval, cultural obligations, or people-pleasing. It's found in Him.

We need to stop confusing familiarity with calling. If abiding in family or familiar relationships is keeping you from abiding in Jesus, God will lovingly prune, and lead you into the full, abundant life He came to give you...where fruit overflows.

John 15:5 (NLT):
I am the vine; you are the branches. Those who remain in me, and I in them, will produce much fruit. For apart from me you can do nothing.

POWER ⚡ SOUL PLUG-IN

Reveal
What is God speaking to me through this chapter?

Reflect
Where in my life have I allowed people, pressure, guilt, or unhealthy access to disturb the peace God wants me to protect?

Respond
What boundary needs to be reset, or established so my life can flourish the way God intended?

Power Move
Choose one boundary you know is needed.
Have the conversation, adjust the access, say no, or create the space needed to guard your peace.

Pray
Lord, give me wisdom to discern what belongs close and what does not.
Help me guard what You have entrusted to me with love and courage.
In Jesus' name, amen.

Declaration
I am not mean for guarding my heart and holding boundaries.
It is wisdom that protects my peace and creates room for God's best to grow.

17

POWER OF DELIVERANCE

2 Corinthians 3:17 (NLT):

For the Lord is the Spirit, and wherever the Spirit of the Lord is, there is freedom.

One night, I was out to dinner when I got a phone call from Kari. I stepped outside the noisy restaurant to hear her better. She explained she was hosting a fundraiser at Mar-a-Lago and then asked, "Brandie, would you open the evening in prayer?"

I almost tripped down the stairs in excitement.

"This is amazing, Kari! I'd love to!"

The day of the event, after a walk on the beautiful sand of Palm Beach, I laid down to rest and pray. I still wasn't sure how I would open my prayer that evening and needed His words to fill my head.

As I lay praying, the Spirit spoke to my heart, saying, JESUS IS THE ULTIMATE FREEDOM FIGHTER.

Yes!

I had the privilege of opening the evening in prayer, and as I did, the presence and power of the Ultimate Freedom Fighter filled the room.

Standing on stage at the President's home, in a ballroom full of freedom fighters, I was humbled. But when the Holy Spirit fell, the prestige of the room and the powerful people in it faded into the background. Because NOTHING compares to Him.

No president truly saves. No general has ever defeated death. No flag raised in triumph could ever measure up to who Jesus is or what He has done.

God loved us so much that He sent His only Son to pay our debt so we could live in freedom, not only forever with Him in the glories of heaven, but here and now. There will always be a war raging in the spirit realm until we are with Him in heaven, and that's why freedom was God's idea from the very beginning.

Colossians 2:15:
But the freedom we receive for eternity is not the same as the freedom we are meant to walk in here and now. What's happening in you matters more than what's happening around you, because that's where the real battle is.

Being saved from eternal hell is not the same as being set free from earthly chains.

For me, that war didn't show up the way I expected. It showed up in my ability to move forward when trying to write this book. I've told these stories in front of PowerSoul for years. So, why was I finding it so hard to dictate the words into pages? Why did my brain freeze and my voice shut down the moment I attempted?

Something wasn't adding up.

About a year and a half earlier, I met Cathy Greer at a speaking event appropriately called "Fight Club." At first, she was just a kind face. But as I tried to write, her name kept coming up in prayer. I felt a strong prompting to call her, but I didn't. I assumed she was more of a high-level business coach, and that wasn't what I needed...or so I thought.

A year later, we were both on the speaking lineup again at the same women's conference. As the speakers all gathered in a prayer circle in preparation, Cathy walked in and came straight to me. I was amazed as she said, "My husband asked what I was excited about tonight, and I said, 'I don't know, but I know I'm supposed to talk to Brandie!'"

I was stunned. "God has been telling me to call you for six months!" I replied.

That night, as we talked, I shared what was going on and how I couldn't seem to finish this book. Not knowing Cathy had a strong prophetic gift and had done ministry around the world for 30 years, I listened as she said, "This year is your coming out party."

Her words were confirmation from above. The Lord had been impressing on me that my seasons were changing and that soon the book would be done.

Cathy became a key part of helping me move forward, especially through what she calls "freedom sessions." A freedom session is where you confront and remove demonic influence operating in your life.

Luke 10:19 (NLT):
Look, I have given you authority over all the power of the enemy, and you can walk among snakes and scorpions and crush them. Nothing will injure you.

During my session, we confronted the areas the enemy was using to hold me back.

WHAT DELIVERANCE REALLY LOOKS LIKE

I know what some of you are thinking…

When people hear the word demon, they immediately go to something out of a movie. Heads spinning, voices changing, full-on chaos like *The Exorcist*. That's not what I'm talking about. Most of the enemy's work in a believer's life is far more subtle and far more strategic.

Demonic strongholds show up in the thoughts you can't seem to shut off, in patterns you keep trying to break but somehow repeat, in reactions or triggers that feel stronger than they should be, and in cycles you find yourself back in even though you love God and genuinely want to move forward.

A believer cannot be possessed by a demon, but they can be influenced, oppressed, and lied to. The enemy doesn't need to own you to affect you. He just needs access. That access often comes through places we don't even realize we've left open. Through wounds that were never healed. Through lies we've believed for so long they feel true. Through trauma, unforgiveness, fear, or patterns we've quietly agreed with over time. Not because you're weak. Not because you don't love God. It's because the enemy looks for agreement. Where there's agreement, there's access.

And when you take that agreement back, that's where freedom starts.

Matthew 8:16:
That evening many demon-possessed people were brought to Jesus. He cast out the evil spirits with a simple command, and he healed all the sick.

Through this process, I began to see clearly that there was more than just natural resistance or procrastination going on. I was battling spirits. A spirit of fear. A spirit of shame. A spirit of control and manipulation. A spirit of rejection.

Yes, even while walking closely with the Lord, the devil still had strongholds on me. The enemy didn't want this book to be born, and he was using familiar spirits to bind me.

With Cathy's help, I commanded those spirits to leave me in the name of Jesus, by the authority Jesus paid for on the cross. And it didn't stop there. What began as my own breakthrough became something God used to equip me to help others through the same kind of freedom sessions I had experienced, watching God do in their lives what He had just done in mine. There are so many people fighting battles they don't even realize they're in.

Jesus paid for your freedom too.

CLOSING THE DOORS

Shortly after, I was still feeling blocked in my writing. This frustrated me, so I took a prayer walk and asked God to show me anything else that might be keeping me stuck. The Holy Spirit whispered, *It's time to stop looking back at your enemies, spiritual and human. Focus on Me.*

I realized I wasn't just focused on the task at hand and obeying God. I had been trying to reverse engineer the outcome instead of letting Him do what only He could do. I had been stuck for so long, fighting off resistance, that I needed to shift my focus back to Him and His power to move through my obedience.

The next week, I fasted coffee (a true sacrifice!) and went for another walk. I asked the Holy Spirit to show me any lingering wounds or lies I had unknowingly partnered with. Almost immediately, memories from every stage of my life came flooding back. Toddler years. Childhood. Adolescence. Adulthood. Times I felt abandoned. Ridiculed. Unchosen.

I rushed home to write them all down. I felt like God Himself was walking me through an exercise to reveal things to me.

Mark 11:25:
But when you are praying, first forgive anyone you are holding a grudge against, so that your Father in heaven will forgive your sins too.

Next to every area of pain I could remember, I wrote the names of the people involved and asked God, "Why did they do this?" Every answer came back to one thing: their own pain.

Suddenly, compassion overwhelmed me. I saw how the ones who had hurt me weren't the enemy. They were just wounded too, fighting the same devil I've been fighting.

Then, in the right margin of my paper, I wrote the names of the people God had sent to love me during these times. Memories came up of mentors, coaches, friends, Matt, my daughters.

Then, I heard the Lord say, *I was there too. In every one of those moments, I was with you. When your heart broke, My heart broke.*

He also prompted me to replace the lies I had believed about myself, with His truth. When I felt abandoned, I wasn't. God calls me His child. When I felt unloved, God called me His beloved...and on and on, I took each lie to the throne and saw the truth that was setting me free. God was using my desperate need to write to draw me closer. As I pursued His voice, He gave me divine revelation of what was blocking my breakthrough.

I thought I had already forgiven all who I needed to, but I realized I was still holding onto things that had hurt me. I was holding onto deep wounds and old disappointments. So, I invited God into all of those places, asked Him to completely heal me, and I let it all go. This experience was purifying.

The next morning, still feeling like I couldn't dictate or write, I became extremely frustrated. "Holy Spirit, what else is keeping me from writing?! Please, Lord! Write Your answer on my mind!"

Then, I saw the words *spirit of manipulation and control.* Scripture calls this witchcraft. And that spirit was tormenting me through other people's word curses over me. Then, in my mind's eye, I saw a spiritual muzzle over my mouth.

That was it. I was mad.

In my kitchen, I began to command those spirits to leave me in the name of Jesus! I warred like I had caught a thief in my house.

"I'm done with you! You don't get to steal from me anymore!"

When I finished, what left me was so tangible that I almost expected to see it flee in physical form. So, I opened the door of my home and commanded those spirits to go.

Then, at that exact moment, a large delivery truck pulled up right in front of my window. I almost couldn't believe my eyes. On the side of the truck was a dragon tearing through paper.

As it drove away, I cried in relief. I was delivered. I was finally free.

Maybe things feel hard because you're in a battle you don't even realize you're in. You think you're failing or don't have what it takes, when in reality there is a devil on your back, weighing you down. A devil in your mind distorting your thoughts. A devil on your chest causing you anxiety.

If you belong to God, the devil wants to torment you. He wants you exhausted, depressed, broke, addicted, angry, sad, alone, and miserable. He wants to steal your testimony and your legacy. He wants the world to see that Christianity doesn't work. He wants to wipe the joy off of your face so you lose all power to lead others to Christ.

And he uses unhealed offense and unforgiveness as a trap.

Ask the Lord to heal your heart where you can't seem to find healing. Leave the past and old offenses at His throne. God is your vindicator. Stop letting the devil take authority over you.

Isaiah 43:18–19:
But forget all that—it is nothing compared to what I am going to do.
For I am about to do something new.
See, I have already begun!
Do you not see it?
I will make a pathway through the wilderness.
I will create rivers in the dry wasteland.

I didn't realize how depressed I was until I was set free.

I didn't realize how oppressed I was until my heavy burdens lifted.

I lived much of my 30's in low-grade depression that I hid pretty well. But I kept pursuing freedom. Then, ten years ago, I read a book that really helped me break free from depression. It was a book of deliverance prayers that changed my life. But like I said, the devil doesn't leave us alone for long, and freedom doesn't come without a fight.

So, I fought. And that night, I wrote seven chapters.

Deliverance is misunderstood and often avoided, and that breaks my heart. Doing a spiritual deep cleaning is vital to breaking free from everything holding you back. And just like cleaning house, freedom is not just something you experience once. It is something you learn to walk in and maintain.

The enemy may be vicious, but in Christ, he is not victorious. So, kick him out of all areas of your life. Take back what he has stolen. Get delivered. Get free.

POWER SOUL PLUG-IN

Reveal
What is God speaking to me through this chapter?

Reflect
Where in my life do I feel stuck, tormented, or trapped in patterns I cannot seem to break on my own?

Respond
What lie, wound, offense, fear, or agreement do I need to bring into God's light so freedom can begin?

Power Move
Ask the Holy Spirit to reveal any area where the enemy has gained influence through pain, lies, or unforgiveness.
Write it down, renounce it, forgive where needed, and invite Jesus to heal and restore that place. If you need help, schedule a freedom session with a trained minister.

Pray
Jesus, thank you for paying for my freedom. Please forgive me for staying offended or not forgiving others the way You've forgiven me. Please expose every lie, heal every wound, and break every chain that has tried to keep me bound. Teach me to walk in the freedom You purchased for me.
In Jesus' name I pray, amen.

Declaration
What held me back does not own me anymore.
Jesus has given me authority, freedom, and power to move forward.

18

POWER TO STAY FREE

1 Peter 5:8 (NLT):

Stay alert! Watch out for your great enemy, the devil. He prowls around like a roaring lion, looking for someone to devour.

Freedom can happen in a moment, but it has to be guarded. Life is messy, and the enemy doesn't disappear just because you've experienced a breakthrough. He watches and waits, looking for the next opportunity to mess with you again.

I've had moments with God where strongholds lifted instantly and I felt completely free, and I've also seen how quickly old thoughts, patterns, and even the same evil oppression can try to come back if I'm not paying attention.

This is where a lot of people get confused. We think if God moved, we're good forever. But we need to remember that until we're with Jesus in heaven, we are in a spiritual war. We must understand that or we will always feel like something is wrong with us.

And this is usually how it shows up.

Sometimes the question isn't whether freedom is available. It's whether you're dealing with something you haven't fully recognized, because there are moments when your life with God is real and sincere, and yet something underneath it still feels off.

When I was dealing with demonic resistance when trying to write this book, it was frustrating and confusing, but it doesn't mean I was failing. And if you are struggling, it doesn't mean you are failing either. Maybe you're just facing something you haven't recognized or haven't learned to confront.

If you're not sure, ask yourself if any of this feels familiar:

You keep circling the same struggle, even after you've prayed about it.

Your thoughts feel louder than they should, condemning, critical, or exhausting.

You start to move forward, and then something in you shuts down.

Your reactions are stronger than the situation calls for.

You feel stuck in patterns you genuinely want to break.

You find yourself isolating or feeling misunderstood.

You avoid prayer or the reading the Word, even when you know it's what you need.

Shame lingers longer than it should, even after you've brought it to God.

If even one of these stands out, don't ignore it.

BE HONEST WITH YOURSELF

One of the most powerful things you can do to stay free is to be honest with yourself. Not harsh or condemning, just honest.

It's easy to talk about the enemy, but it's harder to look at the places where we've been leaving doors open...the habits we haven't let go of, the thoughts we keep entertaining, the conversations we allow, and the patterns we excuse.

Sometimes we want freedom, but we don't want to deal with the sin we keep tolerating.

God meets you when you want to face the truth. Not the version of you that pretends everything is fine, but when you're ready to change and willing to say, "Okay, Lord...where have I partnered with something that isn't from You?"

This kind of honesty is where real freedom begins because it exposes what's actually going on and keeps you from going back into the things that kept you stuck.

Jesus once described what happens when an unclean spirit leaves a person.

Matthew 12:43–45 (NLT excerpt):
When an evil spirit leaves a person, it goes into the desert, seeking rest but finding none. Then it says, 'I will return to the person I came from.' So it returns and finds its former home empty, swept, and in order. Then the spirit finds seven other spirits more evil than itself, and they all enter the person and live there. And so that person is worse off than before.

Jesus is showing it's not enough to just get free. You have to be intentional about what fills your life. It's like kicking a thief out of your house and then leaving the door unlocked so he and his friends can come back and wreak havoc. When you drive evil spirits out, sin and compromise have to go too.

This isn't about living paranoid or constantly looking over your shoulder. It's about closing old doors, living aligned with God, and building new habits.

Remember, you're not doing this on your own. You have the Holy Spirit to empower you and the armor of God to protect you.

Ephesians 6:13–18 (NLT):
Therefore, put on every piece of God's armor so you will be able to resist the enemy in the time of evil. Then after the battle you will still be standing firm. Stand your ground, putting on the belt of truth and the body armor of God's righteousness. For shoes, put on the peace that comes from the Good News so that you will be fully prepared. In addition to all of these, hold up the shield of faith to stop the fiery arrows of the devil. Put on salvation as your helmet, and take the sword of the Spirit, which is the word of God. Pray in the Spirit at all times and on every occasion. Stay alert and be persistent in your prayers for all believers everywhere.

Every piece of God's armor is essential to staying free. Let's talk about each one.

Belt of Truth: Truth matters.

If you don't stay anchored in truth, you will drift back into old thinking and familiar lies, because truth is what keeps you steady when your emotions try to take over.

Breastplate of Righteousness: Guards your heart.

Not perfection or performance, but right standing with God, and when your heart is covered, the enemy's accusations lose their grip.

Shoes of Peace: Steady your steps.

When pressure hits, you don't have to panic or run back to what's comfortable. You can stay grounded in Jesus and move forward in the peace He gives.

Shield of Faith: Blocks what's coming at you.

Fear, doubt, temptation, discouragement...they don't get to land when your faith is active because trust in God protects you.

Helmet of Salvation: Guards your mind.

It reminds you of your identity as God's child, and when that's secure, the enemy has a much harder time messing with your thoughts.

Sword of the Word: It's how you push back.

Speaking truth out loud draws a line and reminds the enemy what he doesn't get access to.

Consistent Prayer: Keeps you connected.

Staying close to God keeps you aware and covered, because when that connection weakens, everything else does too.

Ephesians 6:10–12 (NLT):
A final word: Be strong in the Lord and in his mighty power. Put on all of God's armor so that you will be able to stand firm against all strategies of the devil. For we are not fighting against flesh-and-blood enemies, but against evil rulers and authorities of the unseen world, against mighty powers in this dark world, and against evil spirits in the heavenly places.

So, what do you do when you find yourself struggling again?

Don't panic, just go back to truth. Bring everything into the light and ask the Holy Spirit to show you what's going on and where the door opened. Was it a lie you agreed with, unforgiveness you picked back up, fear you entertained?

Then, ask for forgiveness and close that door. Forgive again if you need to. Release what you picked back up. Break agreement with anything that doesn't align with God's truth, and use your authority.

You don't have to do this perfectly. The closer you stay to God, the quicker you'll recognize when something is off and the easier it is to deal with when something tries to come back.

Don't ignore the enemy and hope he goes away. Don't tolerate what Jesus died to set you free from. Remind the devil he no longer has access to you. Speak the truth and command him to leave, in Jesus' name.

Luke 10:19 (NLT):
Look, I have given you authority over all the power of the enemy, and you can walk among snakes and scorpions and crush them. Nothing will injure you.

POWER ⚡ SOUL PLUG-IN

Reveal
What is God speaking to me through this chapter?

Reflect
Where have I become vulnerable, distracted, or careless in ways that could pull me back into old patterns or old bondage?

Respond
What door needs to be closed again through repentance, truth, forgiveness, or new boundaries so I can remain free?

Power Move
Do a spiritual check-in this week.
Ask the Holy Spirit what feels off or what needs attention.
Then, close the door quickly and return to truth.

Pray
Lord, thank you for the freedom You have given me.
Help me stay alert and strong in every battle.
Give me wisdom to guard my heart and mind. Teach me to answer every lie with Your truth.
Lead me by Your Holy Spirit into complete healing and lasting freedom.
In Jesus' name, amen.

Declaration
What Jesus set free will not return to bondage.
I am equipped, aware, and empowered to stay free from the devil's schemes.

19

POWER OF LOVE

John 3:16:

For God so loved the world that he gave his one and only Son, that whoever believes in him shall not perish but have eternal life.

I can't write "power of love" without hearing Huey Lewis and the News! Yes, I'm THAT old.

Messing with my hair, the stylist's bloodshot eyes looked up at me in the mirror. With scissors in his hand, ready to cut, he asked, "So, what kind of music do you like?"

I'm sure he was expecting 70's or 80's small talk. "I like a lot of genres, but Christian is my favorite."

This sobered him up instantly...

"REALLLLY?" he exclaimed in wonder.

His blue-black hair almost stood up on his head. "How do you get into that stuff?"

"Remember how it felt the first time you fell in love?"

"Sure," he said.

"Before that, love songs didn't matter, right? But then, you fall in love, and a hair-band ballad hits really hard!"

With a half-laugh he turned to mix my color and probably pop a couple Excedrin. I knew he was contemplating my analogy as he painted my hair. I pretended to read my magazine as I thought about it more.

The feelings of first love...my best friend's house, laying on her waterbed next to the Bon Jovi poster on the wall, listening to the boom box that rested on the cheesy mirrored headboard. Dreaming of my crush, as the DJ played late-night dedications, my heart would actually throb!

LOVE MOTIVATES US

Chopping my hair shorter, he started asking questions about how it was having a second baby. My daughter Chloe' was only a few months old, so sitting in silence had been awesome...while it lasted.

"Keep cutting," I said. "I don't have time for my usual head of troll-sized hair." (Halle Berry was rocking a pixie cut, so I thought I could too.)

Going on no sleep and no time for myself, the quiet break was amazing, but I was re-energized just talking about my sweet family.

TRUE LOVE IS WORTHY OF HONOR

God loves us so much that He sent His beloved Son to die in our place. He didn't "kind of" put us first, He gave everything. His Word shows us exactly who He is, what He loves, and how He loves. Page after page, He reveals His heart so we never have to question it. And in it, He doesn't break a single promise.

He expects us to honor Him—not to control us or force relationship, but because we are so loved.

Imagine being madly in love with someone and finding out they feel just meh about you. They keep you around, but they're also flirting with someone on the side. Your husband has a picture of another woman as his screen saver. You ask him about it with tears in your eyes and a pit in your stomach, and he shrugs it off because it doesn't mean anything. "She's cute!"

CUTE?

God doesn't want half of your heart, half of your attention, half of your affection. He wants it all. The Bible says this:

Revelation 3:16:
Because you are lukewarm—neither hot nor cold—I am about to spit you out of my mouth.

This is serious. **Lukewarm love makes Him sick.** He doesn't want us to have divided loyalties, and this reminds me of a story from my own life.

POWER OF CONVICTION

Carved from one piece of wood, a Buddha was gifted to me from my favorite aunt. She brought it back from her travels to Vietnam in the 60's as a flight attendant, and honestly, it made a great necklace holder by my bathroom sink.

I didn't believe in it. I didn't bow to it. So, it seemed harmless.

But one day I felt convicted. Would someone walk into my home and wonder why a Christian had a Buddha in her bathroom? I brushed it off. Then, the conviction grew so strong that I hid it in my closet.

That very night, I listened to a pastor Angela Strong as she ministered live on Facebook. She said, "Someone listening has an idol in your house, and God has been telling you to get rid of it. It's stealing your blessing."

My ears perked up. I knew it was me. Immediately, I grabbed that Buddha and threw it down the trash chute. I felt instant peace, like I had shut a door the enemy had been sneaking through.

God gives us boundaries because He loves us. He's protecting us. Just like you wouldn't want your spouse carrying around a picture of a cute chick, God doesn't want us holding on to idols, objects, or practices that flirt with false gods.

LOVE IS INTENTIONAL. LOVE IS FAITHFUL. LOVE HONORS.

The enemy tries to convince us these things are harmless. Yoga? Just stretching. Crystals? Just décor. Horoscopes? Just for fun. But the truth is, all of these things carry spiritual weight. When we open doors to counterfeit spirituality, we shut the door on intimacy with Jesus. He is jealous for us—not in a petty way, but in a holy way. His jealousy is proof of His fierce love.

Remember, love doesn't leave room for compromise. Lukewarm Christianity is dangerous.

Not all things spiritual are good. Demons are spiritual and know Jesus is Christ!

God's call is clear: *love Me with all your heart, all your soul, all your mind, and all your strength.* He is calling us to love Him and Him alone. He is our source, the Father of spirits, the Father of lights, despite the many ways our culture often tries to remove Him from the equation. Speaking of that...

THE UNIVERSE DOESN'T HAVE YOUR BACK

It was a perfect day in the heart of Laguna Beach. After shrimp tacos on a rooftop deck, my sweet friend Lissette and I wandered into the sweetest boutique. Embellished cowboy hats lined the ceiling, vintage T-shirts, and handmade jewelry.

Everything was priced to move! I told you it was a perfect day...

As I tried to squeeze into the last jumpsuit on the rack, Lissette struck up a conversation with the bohemian babe behind the counter. "This place is so cool!"

"Thank you," said the owner with a twinge of sadness.

We hadn't really noticed the "STORE CLOSING" paint on the windows when we walked in.

Whew! The jumpsuit fit like a glove! I was excited not only because I loved this outfit, but I also wanted to buy something from this kind soul. We both grabbed a couple of bobbles from the ring basket and checked out.

Heading off to our next stop, Lissette filled me in on the young woman's story. Her little store had thrived for seven years but could no longer survive, and she was devastated.

Tug, tug...from the Holy Spirit. *Go back and pray for her.*

So, we walked back and asked if she had a minute to step out front. Delighted and confused, she did. In honest confession, we explained why we came back. "Can we pray for you?"

"Sure. I'm going through such a hard time."

Heads bowed, Lissette held her right shoulder and I her left as her back pressed the glass of her beloved shop. The Holy Spirit did the talking. He wanted her to feel loved and seen.

She started to cry. "Thank you," she mustered as she composed herself.

"Jesus loves you and has a great plan for you. Do you believe in Him?"

"Eh, I believe there is a higher power, and the universe works things out."

I said, "You're right, the highest power of all is the power of Jesus. His name has tremendous power over the entire universe. Let me ask you a question. If you were in a truck that broke down on the side of the road and your best friend came to pick you up, would you thank your friend or the truck?"

God created the universe. He is the driver, and every good thing comes from Him.

James 1:17 (NLT):
Whatever is good and perfect is a gift coming down to us from God our Father...

And the enemy would love for you to call God "the universe" because it strips away the power in the name of Jesus. **There is no spiritual authority in calling God "the universe."**

In her grief, the Lord brought two women from a different state to speak truth and love to her heart. The universe didn't do that...the love of God did.

Romans 8:38–39 (NLT):
And I am convinced that nothing can ever separate us from God's love. Neither death nor life, neither angels nor demons, neither our fears for today nor our worries about tomorrow—not even the powers of hell

can separate us from God. No power in the sky above or in the earth below–indeed, nothing in all creation will ever be able to separate us from the love of God that is revealed in Christ Jesus our Lord.

POWER SOUL PLUG-IN

Reveal
What is God showing me about His love and any places where my heart has been divided?

Reflect
Do I love God with my whole heart, or have I allowed other things to compete for my affection, trust, or attention?

Respond
What is one compromise, distraction, or counterfeit source I need to release so I can love Him more fully?

Power Move
Take inventory of what consumes you most right now.
What gets your time, trust, focus, and affection?
Remove what has been competing with God and replace it with intentional time in His presence.

Pray
Lord, thank you for loving me completely and faithfully.
Show me anything in my life that has taken a place that belongs to You.
Cleanse my heart from compromise and draw me close.
Teach me to love You with all my heart, soul, mind, and strength.
I want You to be first in my life.
In Jesus' name, amen.

Declaration
I am fully loved by God, and my heart belongs to Him.
I will not settle for divided love or counterfeit sources.
Jesus is first in my life, and His love is my greatest power.

20

POWERSOULS CHANGE THE WORLD

2 Corinthians 5:20 (NLT):

So we are Christ's ambassadors; God is making His appeal through us. We speak for Christ when we plead, "Come back to God!"

So many women are asking the same question: What should I do with my life? What is my purpose? And underneath that question is usually pressure.

Am I doing enough? Am I reaching my potential? Am I missing something bigger?

But what if we've been asking the wrong question? What if we're so focused on finding our purpose that we're missing it altogether?

Ephesians 2:10:
For we are God's masterpiece. He has created us anew in Christ Jesus, so we can do the good things He planned for us long ago.

God has given every one of us a mission. Not just pastors, authors, or speakers. If you belong to Christ, your life will hold different assignments in different seasons and one mission that always stays the same.

The world screams:

"MAX OUT! USE ALL OF YOUR POTENTIAL!"

But Jesus didn't live His life trying to "maximize His potential." He lived His life to please the Father. That was the mission. It wasn't to chase influence or impress people. And somehow, in that obedience, everything He did changed the world.

Your assignment isn't to squeeze everything out of yourself or try to become the most impressive version of you. It's so simple: Your daily assignment is to stay close to God and do what He asks. Your ultimate mission is to please Him. That's it.

You don't have to wake up every day trying to figure out your purpose or go in search of yourself on an Eat, Pray, Love tour.

One of the greatest things ever is when I stopped dwelling on myself and woke up with that one mission in mind. You know what happened? My purpose found me!

Every season looks different. What God is asking of you right now may not be what He asked of you five years ago, and it may not be what He asks of you next.

The enemy always wants us living in the past or the future. But asking God for passion—and the ability to be fully present right now, where you are—is a powerful prayer.

Earlier in this book, I shared about my different assignments through different seasons. And through daily obedience, my purpose began to intersect with conversations about culture and even politics. As a radio host and someone leading women through the PowerSoul community, I found myself stepping into conversations I never expected as God led me boldly into new territory.

As my season changed, He began to prepare me, refining my voice and breaking my heart for my next assignment. He stirred a deeper passion in me for His people and how culture, policy, and leadership affect them. Why? Because that's where He wanted me.

For some of you, the most important place you are called to steward right now is your kitchen table. He's asking you to put your phone down and look into the eyes of the little faces across from you, to teach them who God is and help them understand who they are in His Kingdom before they ever leave your house at eighteen. Partnering with God to launch incredible human beings who will love Him and others is no simple task.

That is not small. That is Kingdom work.

For some of you, your assignment is to prepare your home with peace so your husband is welcomed with warmth. It's creating an atmosphere that reflects the love, joy, and presence of God. There was a season when I felt God was asking me to just make sure Matt had clean underwear. (Laundry was never my strong suit. Ha!)

That may not feel like influence to the world, but God sees it differently. What looks small isn't small to God.

Others of you may be entering a completely new season. Maybe, like me, you're now an empty-nester and God is stirring something fresh, giving you new ideas to make an impact outside of your home. Maybe He's prompting you to start a study, be more hospitable, serve your community, or step out of your comfort zone in ways you never imagined.

And for some of you, you're being called to lead—in business, media, ministry, or even run for office. These thoughts may feel intimidating. But if people who love God refuse to participate in shaping culture, we shouldn't be surprised when culture moves further away from Him and greatly affects the next generation.

The world will be shaped by whoever is willing to show up. So, God is calling those who hear Him, love Him, and want to please Him into every arena. We were never meant to hide in pews, my friend. The PowerSoul life doesn't stop at personal freedom. It was always meant to multiply.

Governments alone do not change the world for the better. Hearts transformed by the love of Christ do. And when changed people rise up at home, in business, in schools, in communities, and in places of leadership, their light disrupts darkness. That is how the Kingdom of God moves. That is how territory is taken.

I hope you feel more powerful, qualified, and ready. But none of those things determine your impact. Obedience does.

There are so many directions I could have taken this book and so many topics I didn't fully cover: marriage, parenting, and so much more. But if your heart has truly surrendered to God—and your first priority is to please Him—everything else follows.

When pleasing God comes first, you'll love your spouse better.

When pleasing God comes first, you'll parent with wisdom.

When pleasing God comes first, you'll steward your body well.

When pleasing God comes first, you'll have integrity in business.

When pleasing God comes first, you'll know when to rest and when to move.

When pleasing God comes first, you'll know how to use your unique gifts to fulfill your assignment at the right time.

And in each season of life, you'll stop worrying so much about the things that don't really matter and find joyful purpose in what does.

When we are about God's business, He takes care of ours.

Matthew 6:33 (NLT):
Seek the Kingdom of God above all else, and live righteously, and He will give you everything you need.

The Lord is very clear. When one person lives this way, there is a massive ripple effect. One person can shift the mood...the group...the culture.

So, wherever God has placed you right now, don't undermine it. It matters. Whether it feels big or small or whether anyone else notices, God sees. And He has you there for a season and a reason.

You'll changc your piccc of the world by no longer living from a place of needing love and affirmation but from being SO FULL of the love of Christ that you naturally overflow. That is a life lived in holy ease. When you live this way, you don't have to try to change the world, BUT YOU WILL.

Not because you were chasing purpose or trying to become something, but because you made it your mission to please God, and, PowerSoul, that changes everything.

Matthew 5:14–16 (NLT):
You are the light of the world—like a city on a hilltop that cannot be hidden. No one lights a lamp and then puts it under a basket. Instead, a lamp is placed on a stand, where it gives light to everyone in the house. In the same way, let your good deeds shine out for all to see, so that everyone will praise your heavenly Father.

POWER ⚡ SOUL PLUG-IN

Reveal
What is God speaking to me through this chapter?

Reflect
Am I chasing purpose, recognition, or potential more than I am seeking to please God right where He has placed me?

Respond
What simple act of obedience is God asking of me right now in this season of my life?

Power Move
Ask the Holy Spirit to show you your current assignment, not your whole future.
Then take one faithful step today.
Serve, lead, create, encourage, pray, build, or show up where God has placed you with excellence and love.

Pray
Lord, thank you for creating me with purpose. Please place me exactly where You want me. Help me stop striving for significance and teach me to simply please You. Open my eyes each day to the assignment in front of me. Give me courage to obey, wisdom to steward what You have given me, and love that overflows onto others. Use my life to bring light wherever I go. In Jesus' name, amen.

Declaration
I do not have to chase purpose because I belong to God.
As I seek and obey Him, my life will bear fruit.
I will shine where He has planted me and change the world around me for the better.

21

AFTER THE STORM

Before sunrise, I lace up my shoes and step into the Arizona desert. The world is still asleep, and the sky is waking up with streaks of gold dancing along the horizon as the heat lingers from yesterday's storm. The path is scattered with branches and debris.

It isn't perfect. It's messy. But it's beautiful.

The beauty comes as I sense His nearness. The same Holy Spirit who carried me through storms and refining fires meets me here. The sweat on my skin can't compete with the joy in my spirit. The broken branches beneath my feet remind me of the pruning He's done. The storm clouds remind me that battles will come, but now I don't face them powerless. I face them with confidence in my Savior who continually saves me.

I don't feel rushed or stressed. My desires are different now because I'm different now. I no longer feel the need to run ahead of God toward the next big thing because I've learned something precious: *He is the BIG thing*.

And He's right here. Nothing can take Him away from me.

There is no place I would rather be than in His loving presence. He powers me with His peace. His peace fuels my joy, and His joy strengthens me.

When I married Matt, the final song of the night became a family tradition. We now play it at the end of every family wedding. Arm in arm, everyone gathers in a large circle around the bride and groom, swaying together as the song "I Could Not Ask for More" by Edwin McCain plays.

That song captures this season of my life. Not because it's always easy, but because God is so faithful. After storms of losing my voice, people, and worldly things, and pruning my soul of fruitless desires, His presence remains. And in that presence, I truly could not ask for more.

We only get one life on this planet, but within our one life we live many small ones. There are many chances to learn, to change, to grow, and to move closer to Jesus and His purpose for our lives. I'm so grateful He never gives up on me and that His mercies are new every morning.

As you close these pages, know this with certainty: You are not the same person who opened them. You have been strengthened, clarified, and forged. You have laid down fear, striving, and false identities in exchange for truth, authority, and freedom. What has always been true is now unshakable. You belong to God, and His power lives within you.

You are secure, not in circumstances or in outcomes, but in His presence and love. You are stable, knowing that no matter what comes, you will stand because you are held by the Master of all masters.

So, live rooted, not rushed. Carry the peace you've gained here into every place you go with courage. Walk free, confident, and covered, fully aware that God goes with you.

My prayer is that this book has helped you lift your eyes and press into the One who truly powers your soul. Because the world doesn't need another wimpy Christian. It needs YOU. The new creation God designed. Different. Brave. Set apart.

It needs YOU, filled with the fiery presence of God, making waves, disrupting darkness!

It needs YOU! A PowerSoul, lit from within.

PRAYER

FULL SURRENDER

Romans 5:8:

But God showed his great love for us by sending Christ to die for us while we were still sinners.

If something stirred in your heart while reading this book, don't ignore it. Jesus is calling you. He is not asking you to be perfect. He is asking for your yes. You do not have to have all the answers. You only need to be willing.

If you're ready to fully surrender your life to Him, pray this prayer (on the next page) from your heart:

Jesus, I need You.

I'm done trying to save myself, fix myself, and carry life on my own. I believe You are the Son of God. I believe You died for my sins and rose again in power so I could be forgiven, made new, and truly free.

Today, I turn from my old life and give my whole heart to You.

I invite you to be my Savior and the Lord of my life.

Please, heal what is broken in me

Wash away my sins and renew my mind.

Fill me with Your Holy Spirit and teach me how to follow You.

I surrender what I was never meant to carry and receive the new life You died to give me.

Thank you for loving me, choosing me, and never giving up on me.

My past is broken off and I belong to you.

My future is in Your hands.

Thank you, Lord, for saving me.

In the powerful name of Jesus Christ I pray.

Amen

PowerSoul CLUBHOUSE Scripture

Isaiah 61 is our PowerSoul Scripture because it reveals the heart and mission of Jesus and the identity and freedom He restores to those who follow Him.

Isaiah 61 (NLT):

The Spirit of the Sovereign Lord is upon me,
for the Lord has anointed me
to bring good news to the poor.
He has sent me to comfort the brokenhearted
and to proclaim that captives will be released
and prisoners will be freed.

He has sent me to tell those who mourn
that the time of the Lord's favor has come,
and with it, the day of God's anger against their enemies.

To all who mourn in Israel,
he will give a crown of beauty for ashes,
a joyous blessing instead of mourning,
festive praise instead of despair.
In their righteousness, they will be like great oaks
that the Lord has planted for his own glory.

They will rebuild the ancient ruins,
repairing cities destroyed long ago.
They will revive them,
though they have been deserted for many generations.

Foreigners will be your servants.
They will feed your flocks
and plow your fields
and tend your vineyards.

You will be called priests of the Lord,
ministers of our God.
You will feed on the treasures of the nations
and boast in their riches.

Instead of shame and dishonor,
you will enjoy a double share of honor.
You will possess a double portion of prosperity in your land,
and everlasting joy will be yours.

"For I, the Lord, love justice.
I hate robbery and wrongdoing.
I will faithfully reward my people for their suffering
and make an everlasting covenant with them.

Their descendants will be recognized
and honored among the nations.
Everyone will realize that they are a people
the Lord has blessed."

I am overwhelmed with joy in the Lord my God!
For he has dressed me with the clothing of salvation
and draped me in a robe of righteousness.
I am like a bridegroom dressed for his wedding
or a bride with her jewels.

The Sovereign Lord will show his justice to the
nations of the world.
Everyone will praise him!
His righteousness will be like a garden in early spring,
with plants springing up everywhere.

ACKNOWLEDGMENTS

My God, for being such a good Father. I am amazed and humbled by Your great love.

My Lord, Jesus Christ, for saving me in every single way. There aren't sufficient words to express my gratitude for Your great sacrifice to give me hope, peace, and a future in paradise.

The Holy Spirit, for powering my soul. You graciously lead me to victory, comforting me all along the way. Thank you for walking and talking with me. Your presence is everything.

My husband and very best friend, Matt, for showing me how to love better and being so easy to love. You know me more than anyone and still love me so much that my impossible dreams have become yours. Your exuberant joy, peace, and strength are evidence of God in you. I thank Him every day that you're mine.

My precious daughters, Jadelyn and Chloe', for exhibiting every fruit of the Spirit. Nothing could make me more proud. It is a dream come true to watch you build your lives on Jesus, using the beautiful gifts He has given you.

My honey bunny, Camryn Jade, for lighting a fire under me to get this book done on the day you were born! I hope when you read it, you'll see how Jesus works all things out for good for those who love Him and are called by Him. Always put your faith in Him. He will never let you down.

Cathy Greer, for seeing me, understanding my calling, and speaking life over me and my gifts. A prophet sees a prophet. Your leadership helped push this book into existence. Thank you, dear friend.

Aunt Sandi, for always letting me know how much you care. Your "happy" packages, positivity, hospitality, and encouragement have impacted me more than you'll ever know.

Kellie Smith, Scott Smith, Carrie Liakos, Lissette Lent, Laura Morett, Dan Morett, for being true friends to ride the highs and lows of life with. You bring me so much joy.

Kari Lake, for your courage to stand for truth, no matter the cost. I am so blessed to call you friend.

Angelike and David Norrie, for your faithful friendship and for leading with pure hearts for the Kingdom.

Tina and Brad Hillstrom, for being diamonds in my sky. Your unique talents and fun-loving friendship are gifts to me.

Megan Valentine, for your obedience to Christ in showing up alone, for sitting next to me, and for introducing me to so many incredible women of God.

Joe Courtney, for inspiring me with your story and motivating pep talks.

My parents, for praying over me each night as a child. It was then when the foundation of my faith took root. I am forever grateful.

Joyce Meyer, for powerfully mentoring me through my TV until I knew how to lead myself.

My many brothers and sisters in Christ, for being trusted champions of the faith that I can lean on for prayer. Thank you for strengthening me. Let's keep storming heaven's gates!

Thank you all for being a beautiful part of my story. I love you dearly.

IN REMEMBRANCE

John 8:31–32:

If you abide in my word, you are truly my disciples, and you will know the truth, and THE TRUTH WILL SET YOU FREE.

September 10, 2025

Today, we lost an American hero. At only 31 years old, Charlie Kirk's passion for truth changed the world. He didn't just believe in Jesus; he shared his faith everywhere he went, encouraging the next generation to do the same.

What an extraordinary example he was, using his unique gifts to teach, inspire, and create a movement. He was a revolutionary who stood up to the enemy no matter the cost. Charlie knew some things are worth risking everything, even his life.

But today, he is TRULY FREE in the arms of his Lord. No matter what the enemy meant for harm, Charlie will have eternal victory forever.

And that is not up for debate.

Thank you, Charlie.

RECOMMENDED RESOURCES

These are a few of the books that helped strengthen my understanding of spiritual authority and sharpen my discernment.

- ***Battlefield of the Mind* by Joyce Meyer**

A powerful reminder that the battle often starts in your thoughts and how to take them back.

- ***Clash Between Two Kingdoms* by Angela Strong**

A clear look at spiritual warfare and the authority believers carry.

- ***I Give You Authority* by Charles H. Kraft**

A foundational book on walking in the authority Jesus has already given you.

- ***Defeating Demons* by Stuart Greer**

Practical, grounded insight into deliverance and staying free.

- ***Two Hours to Freedom* by Charles H. Kraft**

A simple and approachable guide to helping people step into freedom.

AUTHOR BIO

Brandie Barclay is the founder of **PowerSoul™**, a movement dedicated to helping women experience God personally and live fully led by the Holy Spirit. A former licensed aesthetician who spent over two decades in the beauty and wellness industry, Brandie made a midlife pivot into ministry and broadcasting, hosting radio shows, and leading community gatherings where Scripture, real talk, and worship collide.

Today, Brandie is a sought-after coach and speaker known for her honest voice, bold perspective, and her ability to make spiritual truths both relatable and transformative. Whether she's hosting a PowerSoul™ "clubhouse" in her Arizona home, mentoring women one on one, or speaking on a national stage, her message is clear: true freedom and purpose come from surrendering to God and walking with Him daily.

Brandie lives in Phoenix, Arizona, with her husband of over 26 years, Matt. They have two adult daughters and one granddaughter, with two more on the way, all of whom inspire everything she does. When she's not teaching or planning the next PowerSoul gathering, you'll find her enjoying life to the fullest with family and friends and pursuing God with her whole heart.

Learn more now at:

www.BrandieBarclay.com

STAY LIT!

Your Next Step Starts Here

To connect with Brandie Barclay for speaking requests, podcast interviews, group and personal coaching, freedom sessions, access to the updated PowerSoul™ music playlist, upcoming PowerSoul™ events, or to donate to PowerSoul™, scan the QR below or visit:

https://linktr.ee/brandiebarclay

If you enjoyed reading *PowerSoul, Lit From Within*, please consider leaving a positive review on Amazon and Goodreads and ordering a copy of for a friend.

www.ingramcontent.com/pod-product-compliance
Lightning Source LLC
LaVergne TN
LVHW010838120826
845149LV00017B/3184

* 9 7 9 8 9 9 5 8 8 1 2 1 6 *